the underground dictionary

by Eugene E. Landy, Ph.D.

SIMON AND SCHUSTER NEW YORK

Copyright © 1971 by Eugene E. Landy
All rights reserved
including the right of reproduction
in whole or in part in any form
Published by Simon and Schuster
A Division of Gulf & Western Corporation
Simon & Schuster Building, Rockefeller Center
1230 Avenue of the Americas
New York, New York 10020

ISBN 0-671-21012-2
ISBN 0-671-20803-9 Pbk.
Library of Congress Catalog Card Number 73–139637
Manufactured in the United States of America

3 4 5 6 7 8 9 10 11 12 13 14 15 16
5 6 7 8 9 10 11 12 13 14 15 16 17 Pbk.

For My People,
Frieda and **Jules**

contents

acknowledgments	9
foreword	11
key to abbreviations	16
guide to pronunciation	17
the underground dictionary	21
numbers	204
symbols	205

acknowledgments

It would be impossible to mention everybody who contributed to the compilation of the terms and definitions found herein. Therefore I would like to thank the many students, patients and friends who went out of their way to eavesdrop here and there and write down every term they heard, usually on matchbook covers, napkins and torn pieces of paper.

I would especially like to thank George L. Beckner, M.D., who compiled a large number of the terms found within, as did Ramón Flores and Dick Kunishima. Dr. William R. Hood of the University of Oklahoma and Dr. Arnold E. Dahlke, Director of Research for the Center for Research in Social Systems of the American University in Washington, D.C., were also extremely helpful. My thanks to the Los Angeles Police Department Narcotics Division and the Los Angeles County Sheriff's Department Narcotics Division for their cooperation.

I would like to thank Bonnie Anderle and Joey Goodman for their persistence and fortitude in the face of what looked like innumerable and undefinable words. They were with me from beginning to end and spent most of their time in defining and redefining terms. They worked specifically in verifying definitions, which included spending a great deal of time in the field. Their work in all areas was outstanding. I would also like to acknowledge Nancy Bloomfield for her work in all phases of the preparation of this manuscript, primarily the typing of it, as well as Chris Hendricks and Fern Pearlstein, who did their share of the typing.

Joan Temple is the one person without whom this dictionary would not have been accomplished. She corrected our English, cross-referenced everything, proofread everything for grammatical, stylistic and

acknowledgments

typing errors, and then proofread it again. Her position as program director for the whole undertaking has placed her in my opinion as responsible for this book as myself. Therefore, publicly allow me to say, "I literally could not have done this dictionary without you, Joan. You have my sincerest gratitude and my deepest respect. You are a wizard."

Finally, to my son Evan, who for months heard nothing but how Daddy couldn't play because he had to work on the book, "Thank you for your understanding, son; now we can go out on the boat."

foreword

No ONE who I've ever known has intentionally started out to write a dictionary and I am no exception. This book, unlike most other works, started out as a therapeutic exercise for a patient of mine.

I had been treating a 25-year-old obese woman who had used heroin and other assorted drugs extensively for more than five years before she entered therapy. I initially hospitalized her for the purpose of withdrawing her from drugs. About two weeks after her hospitalization she began to talk rationally about her use of drugs, methods of obtaining them and the people she encountered during her five-year sojourn through the drug world. As we talked it became obvious to me that both she and I were communicating, we were both talking English, but entirely on a sublevel of the English language. It consisted of slang common to drug users and abbreviations used commonly by police. There were also the new meanings placed on old words by the so-called "hippies" and "dropouts," as well as the "in" sayings that had become popular and common among the younger generation.

I consider myself young and have been dealing with the "young" people for some time (I have become known in Los Angeles as the doper doctor), and I have never had any real difficulty in communicating with them. I speak the language very well. In fact, as I sat there talking to this young woman, it dawned on me that I spoke her language but she couldn't speak mine.

It was at this point I realized that, unlike many of my colleagues, I was a polyglot. I was able to talk to my colleagues in professional language; I was able to talk to non-professional friends; and I was able to

foreword

talk to bikers, colors, connections, cons, dopers, fags, hippies, hookers, musicians, teenyboppers and yippies.

In general, then, I found that I was able to speak to a lot of people, specifically subculture people, with whom my friends and professional colleagues couldn't talk, and that these subculture people could talk to me, whereas they couldn't communicate with my friends or professional peers.

This placed me in the position of an interpreter. Psychologists, psychiatrists and social workers would call me and ask what this or that word meant. I found myself receiving referrals from doctors in general practice, psychiatrists, psychologists, and even from hospitals and clinics where young people were treated and with whom there was trouble communicating.

As my work with these people became more intensive, I was strikingly aware that I had in some aspects become a linguist as a necessary part of being a good therapist. Policemen, principals of schools, teachers, clergymen, as well as parents who couldn't understand or communicate with their children, were continuously in contact with me regarding patients for a more complete and comprehensive understanding of their words, phrases and sentences. A face-to-face interview is often necessary with young people to fully understand what they are attempting to communicate. Not all forms of communication are words. Tones, inflections of voice and even non-verbal gestures are an integral part of the subculture language.

In the process of being a "link" between the two cultures—what has come to be called the underground and the Establishment or overground—I became a collector of words and meanings and had started to compile a list of them for my friends and colleagues in an attempt to save a certain amount of telephone time and explanation. I also found that my ability to speak fluent underground significantly contributed to my access to underground people and places.

The underground language of today was initiated by hard-core drug addicts and criminals of the 1920s and 30s. The purpose for this was that drug addicts and criminals wanted to be sure they were not being infiltrated by an outsider, usually the law. The language became the calling card of many criminals, and instances of the use of this language can be seen in the first crime movies, such as *Underworld* (1927), *Little Caesar* (1930), *Public Enemy* (1931), *Scarface* (1932) and *G-Men* (1935). The popularization and common use of much of that language was prevalent in the 1940s and 50s. The need for a different vocabulary as a code of identification still continues, which explains why the language is constantly changing. If you are an insider (underground person) you are aware of the changes and they are a part of your life. If you are an outsider (overground person) you probably find out about the change in words and meanings by general public use of them, which is usually the time that the underground people have changed them again out of necessity to continue the "in group" process and distinguish the outsider, for he has always been and is still recognized as a threat to their way of life.

For the drug addict the calling card is usually "tracks" (needle marks). In the late 1950s and early 60s, when everybody was under suspicion of drug abuse by injection, the calling card for the drug addict was bare feet, regardless of geographic location or time of year. Why? Because the addict was being examined regularly for needle marks on his arms and he started to "shoot" his drug in the bottom of his feet and then walked around, everywhere, in bare feet so that dirt and the calluses he developed would cover all needle marks. By the mid-1960s, non-drug-using college students as well as soft-drug-using (marijuana and hashish) and occasional hard-drug-using (heroin) college students and hippies were all barefooted, but few were shooting drugs in the soles of their feet. Bare feet became a fad, and when it did, the communication level with the hard-core drug addict changed, for he had stopped using needles in his feet, had put his shoes back on and is currently shooting drugs in parts of the body where evidence is undetectable, such as under the tongue. Meanwhile, the overground now parade around in bare feet, much to the restaurant owners' dismay.

The underground language also created a feeling of cohesiveness, togetherness and belonging with others who share common beliefs, traits and behavior patterns. The uniqueness of the language was in some ways the only uniqueness the individual felt he had, even though for the most part the language was self-degrading and the uniqueness was that of being lower, not as good, basically "freaky." This was and is currently the identity of the underground people and it is reflected in their language.

Therefore, as I spoke to this patient, I knew we could understand each other, but in the course of therapy it would be necessary for her to start to talk to squares who couldn't speak her language. She would have to learn theirs. I asked her, "What does groovy mean?" and with a somewhat surprised look and astonished voice, she responded, "Groovy means groovy, man."

"Yeah, I know, but what does it mean?"

She sat, bewildered, thought and finally said, "Wow."

"It must mean more than that."

"You know what it means."

"Yes, I do. I can explain it. Can you?"

She found it impossible and left with instructions to write an explanation of the word "groovy" before our next visit. I also asked her to define any other words, phrases or exclamations that she used regularly, such as wow, yeah, man, you know. She returned with the simplest form of written explanations and I requested that she write more detailed explanations and expand the meanings of the few words to their fullest extent.

These words of that patient (who today is a non-drug-using, thin executive secretary) were the beginning of this book. They were the start of a therapeutic exercise that brought into focus the fact that greater than the generation gap was the communication gap that existed between parent and child, or more specifically the people of the underground and the overground.

This book was written for all people with the hope that an understanding of the language will fill the chasm in the communication gap and will work toward neither an underground nor an overground but rather a common ground for all people. I think this starts with being able to talk, communicate and understand. Therefore, if you don't understand a word, you can now look it up. If it makes sense to you, if you feel comfortable with it, then use the word; if not, don't. But at least you will know what other people are talking about, regardless of whether you are an underground, overground or common-ground person.

Los Angeles, Calif.   E.E.L.
January 1971

key to abbreviations

adj.	adjective	ie.	that is
adv.	adverb	n.	noun
a.k.a.	also known as	prep.	preposition
eg.	for example	v.	verb

TERMS SPECIAL TO PARTICULAR SUBCULTURES
- (B)   Blacks
- (d)   drug users
- (h)   homosexuals
- (m)   motorcycle groups
- (med) medical, scientific or chemical personnel
- (mu)   musicians
- (p)   prisoners and police
- (pr)   prostitutes

These abbreviations of various subcultures follow the part of speech denotation when the term being defined is generally peculiar to only *one* subculture In the case of a word having more than one definition and being used by more than one group, these abbreviations follow the number of the definition.

Words in Spanish are so noted, with pronunciation

CROSS REFERENCES

a.k.a. (also known as) follows the definition of a word with one or more slang words that are interchangeable with the one being defined. Each has its own alphabetical listing.

"See" refers the reader to one or more general terms to which the slang word is related. These terms are usually not slang but are included so that a broader, more elaborate definition can be supplied.

guide to pronunciation

Pronunciation is indicated in parentheses immediately after the main entry. If no pronunciation is given, the word is pronounced as in everyday English.

Symbol	*Key Word*
a	fat
ā	ape
ah	father
ɔ	fall, law
e	ten
ē	even, see
i	hit
ī	bite
o	horn, fork
ō	go
oo	book
o͞o	tool
oi	oil, boy
ou	out
u	up, cut
ū	use, cute
ə (always unstressed)	ago, agent, sanity, comply, focus
ər	turn, worm
g	get
j	joy, giant
y	yet
ch	chin
sh	she
th	thin, thank
ᴅ̵	then, father
zh	azure, leisure

the underground dictionary

a

A *n.* (d) **1.** Amphetamine; an upper. See AMPHETAMINE. **2.** LSD; acid. Comes from first letter of acid. See HALLUCINOGEN; LYSERGIC ACID DIETHYLAMIDE.

ab *n.* (d) Abscess.

abbot *n.* (med) Nembutal; a downer. Sleeping compound in capsule form, yellow in color. Word is derived from the pharmaceutical company that manufactures it. See BARBITURATE; NEMBUTAL.

A-bomb *n.* (d) Cigarette made of a mixture of drugs, usually marijuana and heroin or opium and hashish. See DUST.

Acapulco gold (ah-kah-pōōl'-kō gold) *n.* (d) Very high quality marijuana grown near Acapulco, a tropical resort town in Mexico. Called gold because of its golden beige color. **a.k.a.** gold, golden leaf. See MARIJUANA; PANAMA GOLD.

AC-DC *adj.* Bisexual; both homosexual and heterosexual activities or involvements; refers to both male and female. Comes from abbreviations of alternating current and direct current—an electrical term. **a.k.a.** bi. See SWITCH HITTER.

ace *n.* (d) Marijuana cigarette. See MARIJUANA CIGARETTE. *adj.* Superior—eg. *That's really ace!*

ace in *v.* **1.** Maneuver one's way into a lucrative situation. **2.** Understand; become aware—eg. *I aced in on their conversation.*

acid *n.* (d) LSD. See HALLUCINOGEN; LYSERGIC ACID DIETHYLAMIDE.

acid freak *n.* (d) Habitual user of LSD; one who uses LSD exclusively or predominantly and subscribes to other customs of the LSD cult.

acid funk *n.* (d) **1.** Music. Comes from acid, which means LSD. **2.** LSD-induced depression.

acid head

acid head *n.* (d) Frequent user of LSD. Users of LSD refer to one another as acid heads. **a.k.a.** A-head. See HEAD.

acid lab *n.* (d) Any place where hallucinogenic drugs are produced illegally, eg., in a school chemistry lab or a garage.

acid mung *n.* (d) State and feeling of having a very oily face when one is on an acid (LSD) trip. It does not always occur. See MUNGY.

acid pad *n.* (d) Place to take drugs. Can be any kind of place: an apartment, a cave. **a.k.a.** launching pad, shooting gallery. See PAD.

acid rock *n.* (d) Psychedelic music. Comes from acid, which means LSD. It emphasizes electronic sounds; has a very prominent beat, repeated sounds. It is sometimes atonal and amelodic, often loud. It is associated with the feelings and effects of an LSD experience. Acid rock is considered to be the musical equivalent of an LSD-induced state. It has more significant meaning when listened to under the influence of LSD. **a.k.a.** freak rock. See HARD ROCK; PSYCHEDELIC.

acid test *v.* (d) Do something extra to enhance a mood or experience (generally the LSD experience), usually done at parties—eg. *I'm going to acid test my apartment with strobe lights.*

ácido (*Spanish* ah'-sē-dō) *n.* Acid; LSD. See HALLUCINOGEN; LYSERGIC ACID DIETHYLAMIDE.

action n. Activity or excitement of any kind—*eg. Where's the action?*

A.D. *n.* (d) Drug addict. Comes from the fact that D.A. commonly stands for District Attorney so drug takers reverse the initials to avoid confusion.

addict *n.* **1.** One who is physiologically or psychologically addicted to drugs. **2.** (d) Usually refers to one who is addicted to heroin.

aerosol *n.* (d) Aerosol can whose contents can be inhaled to obtain a high. Contents sprayed into balloon or paper bag, and then inhaled. *Warn-*

ing: if sprayed directly into mouth, lethal. See GLUE, GLUE SNIFFING.

Afro *n.* (B) Natural Black hair style; hair not straightened but left in its natural curly state and styled; also worn by whites with curly hair. **a.k.a.** natural. See PROCESS. *adj.* Prefix denoting Black—eg. *Afro-American.*

A-head *n.* (d) **1.** Frequent, habitual, often exclusive user of amphetamines. **2.** Acid head; one who takes LSD. See HEAD.

A.K. *n.* Ass kisser. **a.k.a.** Kiss ass. See ASS KISSER; BROWN NOSE; KISS SOMEONE'S ASS; KISSY.

alba de narco (*Spanish* ahl'-bah dā nahr'-kō) *n.* **1.** Narcotics agent; cop. **2.** Expression meaning "Watch out!"

Alice B. Toklas *n.* Brownie with marijuana baked in it. Alice B. Toklas was female companion, lover and chef to Gertrude Stein, poet of the 1920s. They lived in Paris. In 1929 Alice B. Toklas published *The Alice B. Toklas Cook Book.* The book is full of delicacies and under the dessert section is a recipe for fudge with cannabis (marijuana). In the 1960s a movie called *I Love You Alice B. Toklas* was made, inspired by that fudge recipe. The movie is about someone who gets high for the first time on brownies made with marijuana.

alyo *n.* (p) Agreement between criminal and police leading to protection and safety for the criminal.

amock *n.* (d) User of marijuana. Comes from the Malay word *amoq*, which means to kill. **a.k.a.** amuck.

amphetamine (am-fe'-tə-mēn) *n.* (med) A stimulant that is swallowed or injected. Stimulates the central nervous system. It is medically used for the treatment of narcolepsy to counteract the effects of depressant drugs and to depress appetite. It is also used psychiatrically in the treatment of psychoses. Amphetamines are not physically addictive; there are no withdrawal symptoms except a drop in energy level. They do cause psychic dependence, extreme restlessness or nervousness, tremor, dryness of mouth, tachycardia, loss of appetite, insomnia and feelings of increased initiative. They are often used by students to stay awake for long periods of time. They do not improve performance. Sustained abuse leads to malnutrition, excessive fatigue, severely impaired judgment and psychosis resembling paranoid schizophrenia. The commercial preparations most commonly used by drug abusers are Benzedrine, Dexedrine, Methedrine, Desoxyn, Eskatrol. **a.k.a.** A, bam, booster pill, chalk, copilot, driver, football, forward, garbage, G.B., goofball, green dragon, jelly baby, jolly bean, leaper, lid popper, lift pill, peach, pep pill, sparkle plenty, speed, sweet, thrust, truck driver, up, upper, uppie, wake up, white, whitie, zoom. See BENZEDRINE; BIPHETAMINE; DESOXYN; DEXEDRINE; ESKATROL; METHEDRINE; METHYL DI-AMPHETAMINE; WYAMINE.

ampule (am'-py$\overline{oo}$l) *n.* (med) Glass container in which liquid drugs are dispensed. **a.k.a.** jug.

amuck See AMOCK.

amy *n.* (d) Amyl nitrite. See AMYL NITRITE.

amyl nitrite (am'-il nī'-trīt) *n.* (med) Stimulant commonly used as an ejaculatory inhibitor to prolong intercourse and orgasm; creates distortions of perceptions and a feeling of expansion in the head; an upper. It is medically used for treatment of coronary conditions and asthma. It is dispensed in a cloth-covered plastic capsule that must be broken to inhale. It takes effect in 30 seconds and lasts for two to three minutes. It can be taken only by inhalation. **a.k.a.** amy, pearls, popper, popsie, snapper.

Amytal (am'-i-təl) *n.* (med) (amabarbital; Eli, Lilly and Co.) Moderately long-acting barbiturate; a downer. It is medically used as a sedative and for the relief of anxiety and tension. Comes in tablet form. **a.k.a.** blue, blue angel, blue heaven. See BARBITURATE.

ándale (*Spanish* ahn'-dah-lā) Expression meaning (1) yes, I agree; (2) let's go; (3) do the thing that you have started to do; continue toward a goal. **a.k.a.** ódale.

angel dust *n.* (d) A drug used to get high. The drug itself is legal, but using it to get high is not. It is a tranquilizer used for hogs. It is sprayed on mint leaves; they are then dried, rolled tight and smoked. **a.k.a.** hog.

antsy *adj.* Nervous; bugged; restless. Comes from "ants in your pants." **a.k.a.** yantsy.

apart *adj.* In a state of confusion; opposite of together. See TOGETHER.

A.R. *n.* (p) Armed robbery. Term used by prisoners and also officially used by police when booking someone.

arasqua See ARATHWA.

arathwa *n.* Amazon basin hallucinogen used by shamen to induce delusion of being a python, eagle or jaguar (effects particular to that culture); being used today primarily by intellectual drug users. Effects last 36 hours. **a.k.a.** arasqua. See HALLUCINOGEN.

around the world *n.* (pr) Act of kissing, sucking and licking the penis, testicles and anus; a common request made by men who frequent prostitutes. See FREAK TRICK.

arreador (*Spanish* ah-rā-ah-dor') *n.* Seller of drugs. See PUSHER.

artillery *n.* (d) Equipment used for preparing and injecting drugs. See FIT.

ass hole *n.* **1.** Anus. **a.k.a.** round eye. **2.** Stupid, irritating person.

ass kisser *n.* One who attempts to gain approval and acceptance by being exceptionally nice. **a.k.a.** A.K., kiss ass. See BROWN NOSE; KISS SOMEONE'S ASS; KISSY.

Asthmador *n.* Powder, often in cigarette form, for

inhalation therapy with asthmatics. It contains stramonium and belladonna; both are toxic and produce hallucinations when taken in large quantities.

Augustus Owsley. See OWSLEY, AUGUSTUS.

aunt emma *n.* (d) Morphine. See MORPHINE.

auntie *n.* (h) An aging homosexual.

automobile See CAR.

ax *n.* (mu) Musical instrument; commonly used for guitar.

azul (*Spanish* ah-sool') *n.* Policeman; cop. Literal translation is "blue," from the color of the policeman's uniform. **a.k.a.** chota, tombo. See POLICEMAN.

b

B *n.* (d) Unit of measurement for the sale of marijuana; sufficient marijuana to fill one penny matchbox. **a.k.a.** bee. See QUANTITIES OF DRUGS.

babe *n.* Female. See FEMALE.

baby *n.* **1.** (d) Marijuana. See MARIJUANA. **2.** (B) Form of address to a male or a female. **3.** Female. See FEMALE.

back door *n.* Anus; used in referring to anal intercourse between male and female or between males—eg. *He fucked her in the back door.*

backwards *adj.* Usually refers to tranquilizing effect of slowing down after taking a tranquilizer.

Bactine bag *n.* Bactine, a liquid antiseptic, put into a plastic bag and inhaled. It can cause death due to suffocation from the plastic bag. It is commonly used by 8th, 9th and 10th graders. Bactine can be very dangerous when inhaled directly from the aerosol can because the chemical in the can freezes the larynx.

bad *adj.* **1.** Can be either positive or negative—eg. *A bad scene* can mean an unfortunate experience or a very good experience. **2.** Used to describe a tough, mean person—eg. *That guy is really bad.*

bad bundle *n.* (d) **1.** Heroin that has been exposed to moisture, resulting in a somewhat deteriorated condition, and sold at a lower price. **2.** Heroin that has been cut, diluted. See CUT.

bad go *n.* (d) Small amount of drugs for the price paid.

bad scene *n.* Unpleasant experience; disappointment.

bad self See GO ON WITH YOUR BAD SELF.

bad trip *n.* (d) Negative reaction of panic, fear, depression or anxiety that can result from the use of any drug, especially LSD. **a.k.a.** bum bend, bum kicks, bum trip, down trip.

badge *v.* Appear to be an authority. *n.* Too small an amount of a drug for the money paid.

bag *v.* (d) Place drugs or marijuana in a bag. **a.k.a.** deck up. *n.* **1.** Person's own way of life—eg. *His bag is jazz.* **a.k.a.** bit, story. **2.** Situation or personal problem. **a.k.a.** bit, thing. **3.** (d) Packet of narcotics—eg. *I need a bag of heroin.* **a.k.a.** bindle, bird's eye, biz, bolsa, bundle, deck, foil, packet, paper. See DIME BAG; NICKEL BAG; QUANTITIES OF DRUGS. **4.** Female. See FEMALE.

bagman *n.* (d) Person who sells drugs. Comes from bag, which means to place drugs in a bag or the packet of drugs itself. See PUSHER.

bale *n.* (d) Seventy-five to 500 pounds of marijuana. Comes from compressing marijuana into bales in a fashion similar to baling hay or alfalfa. When stored this way spoilage is retarded.

ball *v.* **1.** Have sexual intercourse—eg. *Did you ball her last night?* See COPULATE. **2.** Absorb a narcotic via genital mucosa. *n.* A good time—eg. *We had a ball.*

balloon *n.* (d) Ordinary toy balloon used for storing or carrying heroin.

balls *n.* **1.** Testicles. See TESTICLES. **2.** Guts; courage; daring; impulsiveness. When describing a man, it implies strength and masculinity—eg. *He's got balls.* When describing a female, it can have a negative or positive connotation. **a.k.a.** cojones, hair, juice. See BALLSEY.

ballsey *adj.* Very forward, aggressive and impulsive. When used to describe an aggressive female it can have a negative or positive connotation, but it is always complimentary to males. See BALLS.

bam *n.* (d) **1.** Mixture of stimulant and depressant. May have come from *b* from barbiturate plus *am* from amphetamine. **2.** Amphetamine. See AMPHETAMINE.

bang *v.* **1.** Insert finger into vagina with repetitive movement for sexual stimulation, simulating intercourse. **a.k.a.** finger fuck. **2.** Have sexual intercourse—eg. *I'm going to bang that girl.* See COPULATE. *n.* (d) An injection of a narcotic. See INJECTION.

bar *n.* (d) Marijuana or hashish mixed with water and honey or sugar so it will harden into a solid block. This procedure facilitates shipping and sale of the drug. **a.k.a.** brick.

barb *n.* (d) Barbiturate; a downer; depressant. May be swallowed or injected. See BARBITURATE.

barbiturate *n.* (med) Commonly known as a sleeping pill. Barbiturates are a leading mode of suicide. If taken and not followed by sleep, euphoria, mental confusion and stimulation occur; after a time, these effects turn into drowsiness, vagueness, blurred vision, lack of coordination and eventual unconsciousness (see CRASH). With abuse, they can be physically and psychologically addictive. The withdrawal is more severe than withdrawal from heroin: the symptoms are weakness, rise in pulse and temperature, shaking, epileptic-type seizures and convulsions. Medically, barbiturates are used to induce sleep, for treatment of epilepsy and high blood pressure, and for calming effect in mental disorders. The commercial preparations most commonly used by drug abusers are Seconal, Nembutal and Tuinal. **a.k.a.** barb, down, downer, downie, goofball, Mexican jumping bean, peanut, phenie, sleeper, stum. See AMYTAL; NEMBUTAL; SECONAL; TUINAL.

bark *v.* Talk loudly; scream; yell—eg. *Don't bark at me.*

barrel *n.* (d) Barrel-shaped tablet that contains LSD.

bat *n.* **1.** Prostitute. See PROSTITUTE. **2.** Drunk binge—eg. *He went on a bat.*

bato (*Spanish* bah'-tō) *n.* Male; guy; male who is tough; gang member.

bato loco (*Spanish*) *n.* Guy who will do anything; loco means crazy.

bato marijuano (*Spanish*) *n.* Male who uses marijuana.

bato narco (*Spanish*) *n.* Male who uses narcotics.

bazoom *n.* Female's breast. Term used in the Army particularly. See BREAST.

B-bomb *n.* (d) Benzedrine inhaler that has excessive Benzedrine content. It was removed from the market in 1949 and replaced with Benzedrex Inhaler (Smith, Kline & French Laboratories), which contains no Benzedrine.

B.C. *n.* Birth control. See CONTRACEPTIVE.

Be aware Slogan meaning to be on the alert for Federal narcotics officers or to be in touch with what is going on around one. Originally from a Berkeley art poster.

be down on *v.* Be angry at, disapproving of—eg. *I'm really down on him.*

be hung up on See HUNG UP ON.

be in *n.* Gathering of people in order to partake of spontaneous activities. See LOVE IN.

be in a high place *v.* Be in a good mood; be happy.

be on to *v.* Find out about something or someone; become aware of—eg. *I'm on to you.*

beads *n.* Smooth beads strung with knots between them, ranging in size from small to large. They are inserted, usually with the larger bead first, bead by bead into the anus during sexual play or intercourse and pulled out rapidly upon reaching climax. This intensifies the climax. The insertion is usually done while engaging in fellatio. These beads originated in the Orient. **a.k.a.** Japanese beads.

beam, on the See ON THE BEAM.

bean *n.* **1.** Derogatory term for a Mexican. **a.k.a.** beaner. **2.** (d) Benzedrine. See AMPHETAMINE; BENZEDRINE.

beaner *n.* Derogatory term for a Mexican. **a.k.a.** bean.

bear *n.* **1.** Ugly female. **2.** Something very difficult.

beat *v.* Cheat someone out of something. See CON; CON GAME.

beat off *v.* Masturbate. See MASTURBATE.

beat the dough *v.* (d) Run out with the money, not giving the buyer the drugs.
beat the 8 ball *v.* Take heroin.
beat the meat *v.* Masturbate (male). See MASTURBATE.
beautiful *adj.* All-purpose term of approval; can be used as an exclamation—eg. *Beautiful!*
beautiful people *n.* **1.** Enlightened, aware people; people in the know. **2.** People in tune with the hippy, modern scene of flowers, love and peace. **3.** The so-called jet set.
beaver *n.* **1.** The area around the vagina; pubic region. Comes from the view of the pubic hair, which resembles the furriness of a beaver. See BUSH. **2.** Vagina. See VAGINA. **3.** Female. See FEMALE.
beaver shot *n.* **1.** A look at a woman's vagina (or underpants) because of the way she is sitting. **a.k.a.** split beaver, spread beaver. **2.** A photograph of a woman with her legs spread, showing the vagina and pubic area. **a.k.a.** split beaver, spread beaver.
bee *n.* (d) Unit of measurement for the sale of marijuana; sufficient marijuana to fill one penny matchbox. **a.k.a.** B. See QUANTITIES OF DRUGS.
been had *adj.* **1.** Been taken advantage of. **2.** Has had sexual intercourse. **3.** Arrested.
behind it *adj.* **1.** Involved with; engrossed in—eg. *He was really behind it.* **2.** Aware of; understanding. *prep.* **1.** Because of—eg. *I got mad behind it.* **2.** In back of; in addition to—eg. *Behind my high, I thought of him.*
bell rope *n.* Penis. See PENIS.
belladonna *n.* (med) A wild plant which if ingested can cause delirium or death. Used to get high.
bend *v.* Do something you don't want to do, perhaps being angry about it—eg. *He bent to it.*
benny *n.* (d) Benzedrine. See AMPHETAMINE; BENZEDRINE.

bent *adj.* **1.** Disturbed; angry; irrational. **a.k.a.** bent out of shape, out of shape, pushed out of shape. **2.** (d) Under the influence of a drug. **a.k.a.** bent out of shape. See LOADED. **3.** Gay, homosexual.
bent out of shape. See BENT.
benz *n.* (d) World War II slang for Benzedrine. See AMPHETAMINE; BENZEDRINE.
Benzedrine (ben'-zə-drēn) *n.* (med) (Smith, Kline and French Laboratories) Stimulant that creates an artificial feeling of excitement and a surge of power, inhibits sleep; an upper. It is medically used for weight reduction. **a.k.a.** bean, benny, benz, goofball, hi-ball, pep pill, white. See AMPHETAMINE.
benzine *n.* Substance widely used as a cleaning fluid. Has been inhaled for its intoxicative effects.
benzodiazepine *n.* (med) Chemical whose derivatives are used in minor tranquilizers such as Librium and Valium.
Bernice *n.* (d) Cocaine. See COCAINE.
best piece *n.* Girl friend; wife.
better half *n.* **1.** Boy friend or girl friend. **2.** Husband or wife. See GIRL FRIEND; WIFE.
bhang *n.* Marijuana; the resin that is taken off the leaves of the plant. **a.k.a.** bhang ganjah. See MARIJUANA.
bhang ganjah (bang gahn'-jə) *n.* Marijuana; the resin that is taken off the leaves of the plant. **a.k.a.** bhang. See MARIJUANA.
bi (bī) *adj.* Bisexual; both homosexual and heterosexual activities or involvements. Refers to both male and female. **a.k.a.** AC-DC. See SWITCH HITTER.
big bloke *n.* Cocaine. See COCAINE.
big brown eye *n.* Female's breast. See BREAST.
big chief, the *n.* (d) **1.** Mescaline. See HALLUCINOGEN; MESCALINE. **2.** LSD. See HALLUCINOGEN; LYSERGIC ACID DIETHYLAMIDE.
big D *n.* (d) LSD. See HALLUCINOGEN; LYSERGIC ACID DIETHYLAMIDE.

big H *n.* **1.** (d) Heroin. See HEROIN. **2.** (p) Big house (jail). Usually refers to San Quentin Prison.

big John *n.* (d) Policeman. See POLICEMAN.

big time *n.* **1.** (p) Time in state prison. **2.** Sexual intercourse. See COPULATION. **3.** (d) Using heroin or morphine—eg. *He's in the big time. adj.* Having a high status position—eg. *He's big time.*

bike *n.* Motorcycle.

bike pack *n.* (m) **1.** Motorcycle gang. **2.** Long trip on motorcycles. See BIKE.

biker *n.* **1.** One who enjoys riding a motorcycle and does so frequently. **2.** A member of a motorcycle group or gang. See BIKE.

bim *n.* (p) Policeman—eg. *The bims went bam and took me to the slams.* (The police arrested me and took me to jail.) See POLICEMAN.

bindle *n.* (d) Envelope containing morphine, cocaine or heroin. See BAG.

Biphetamine *n.* (med) (d- and dl-amphetamine; Strasenburgh Laboratories) Stimulant that affects the central nervous system. Tablet has a white top and a black bottom. **a.k.a.** black and white, black beauty. See AMPHETAMINE.

bird *n.* **1.** Female. See FEMALE. **2.** Term for the middle finger when raised alone, which means Fuck you—eg. *That guy gave me the bird.* **a.k.a.** bone. See FUCK; FUCK YOU. **3.** Male who would be considered a bore and not "in with the times." **4.** (B) Fried chicken.

birdie powder *n.* (d) Mixture of heroin and morphine.

bird's eye *n.* (d) Small packet of narcotics. See BAG.

birra (*Spanish* bē'-rah) *n.* Beer or any intoxicating drink.

bit *n.* **1.** Activity—eg. *What's your bit?* = *What are you doing?* **a.k.a.** thing. **2.** Person's own way of life or style of behavior—eg. *My bit is drugs.* **a.k.a.** bag, story. **3.** Situation or personal problem. Now being used less in favor of bag—eg. *What's his bit?* **a.k.a.** bag, thing.

bitch

bitch *v.* Complain—eg. *Stop bitching.* *n.* **1.** Female who is mean, selfish, cruel, malicious, deceiving. **a.k.a.** cunt. **2.** Female. See FEMALE. **3.** Good thing or person; person good at something—eg. *He's a bitch of a player.* **4.** Very difficult or tedious thing —eg. *That test is going to be a bitch.*

bitchen (bi'-chən) *adj.* Fantastic; great; very groovy —eg. *That's bitchen!* See GROOVY.

bitchy *adj.* Malicious; spiteful; complaining.

biz *n.* Small quantity of narcotics. See BAG.

Black *n.*, *adj.* Negro. Originated in the Negro community with the rise of racial pride; a common slogan is Black is beautiful.

black and white *n.* **1.** (d) 12.5-mg. capsule of an amphetamine and a sedative. **a.k.a.** black and white minstrel, domino, minstrel. See SPEEDBALL. **2.** (d) Biphetamine. Comes from dual color of capsule. **a.k.a.** black beauty. See AMPHETAMINE; BIPHETAMINE. **3.** Los Angeles police car. Comes from black-and-white paint job of the car. **4.** Policeman. See POLICEMAN. **5.** (B) Two policemen riding together, one Black and one white.

black and white minstrel *n.* (d) 12.5-mg. capsule of an amphetamine and a sedative. **a.k.a.** black and white, domino, minstrel. See SPEEDBALL.

black beauty *n.* (d) Biphetamine. Capsule is black and white. **a.k.a.** black and white. See AMPHETAMINE; BIPHETAMINE.

black bomber *n.* (d) 20-mg. capsule of an amphetamine and a sedative. See SPEEDBALL.

black gungi (blak gun'-jē) *n.* (d) Form of marijuana grown in India and smuggled into the United States. See MARIJUANA.

black light *n.* Ultraviolet (purplish-colored) light that makes fluorescent material glow in the dark, used to achieve a psychedelic effect. See PSYCHEDELIC.

Black Panthers *n.* Militant organization of Blacks who are engaged in promoting the welfare of Black people; they believe in armed self-defense and armed revolution.

black pill *n.* (d) Pellet of opium placed in a pipe and smoked. See OPIUM.

black Russian *n.* (d) Dark-colored hashish. See HASHISH.

black stuff *n.* (d) Opium. See OPIUM.

black wings *n.* (m) Symbol worn on jackets of members of white motorcycle gangs to signify having had sexual relations with a Black person.

blah, blah, blah Expression used in conversation to avoid explaining something in detail; means et cetera, et cetera, et cetera.

blank *n.* (d) **1.** Quantity of powder, such as talcum powder, baking powder, scraped chalk, baking soda or milk sugar, sold to an addict as heroin. **a.k.a.** dummy, turkey. **2.** Extremely low grade drug.

blast *n.* **1.** A very good time—eg. *This party is a blast.* **2.** (d) Long, deep puff of a marijuana cigarette—eg. *Here, take a blast.* **3.** (d) Strong effect from a drug.

blast a joint *v.* (d) Smoke marijuana. **a.k.a.** blast a stick, blow, blow a stick, blow hay, blow it.

blast a stick *v.* (d) Smoke marijuana. See BLAST A JOINT.

blast party *n.* (d) Gathering for the purpose of taking marijuana; marijuana party. **a.k.a.** blasting party, pot party. See BLAST.

blasted *adj.* Under the influence of drugs or alcohol. See LOADED.

blasting party See BLAST PARTY.

block *n.* (d) Quantity of compressed hashish. **a.k.a.** bar, brick.

blocked *adj.* Under the influence of a drug, alcohol, or both. See LOADED.

bloke, big See BIG BLOKE.

blood bread *n.* Money received by selling blood to blood banks, usually used to buy narcotics. **a.k.a.** red bread. See MONEY.

blow *v.* **1.** (d) Smoke marijuana. See BLAST A JOINT. **2.** Orally copulate the penis. See FELLATIO; ORAL

COPULATION. **3.** Leave. See LEAVE. **4.** (mu) Play an instrument. **5.** Perform. **6.** Talk. **a.k.a.** rap.

blow a stick *v.* Smoke marijuana. See BLAST A JOINT.

blow hay *v.* Smoke marijuana. See BLAST A JOINT.

blow hole *n.* Hole in wall between toilet stalls in men's rooms. Comes from the use of these holes for oral copulation between males. See BLOW JOB; ORAL COPULATION.

blow it *v.* **1.** (d) Smoke marijuana. See BLAST A JOINT. **2.** Fail at an endeavor—eg. *I blew that test.* **3.** Lose control of one's actions. **4.** Release tension.

blow it off *v.* Drive very fast in a car. **a.k.a.** blow it out, get in the wind.

blow it on him *v.* Have someone arrested.

blow it out *v.* Drive very fast in a car. **a.k.a.** blow it off, get in the wind.

blow job *n.* Oral copulation of the penis. **a.k.a.** fellatio, pipe job. See BLOW HOLE; CUNNILINGUS; ORAL COPULATION.

blow snow *v.* (d) Inhale cocaine. See SNIFF.

blow the bag *v.* (d) Sniff or inhale any toxic ingredient such as glue. **a.k.a.** horn, sniff, snort.

blow your cool *v.* **1.** Lose control of your emotions or composure. **2.** Lose your temper. See COOL.

blow your mind *v.* **1.** Be totally overcome by an idea, place, thing or person—eg. *That movie will blow your mind.* **2.** (d) Take an LSD trip and never return to normal; have an emotional breakdown, never returning to normal.

blue *n.* (d) **1.** Dexamyl. See AMPHETAMINE; BARBITURATE; DEXAMYL. **2.** Amytal; a downer. See AMYTAL; BARBITURATE. **3.** Pill of the amphetamine type. See AMPHETAMINE.

blue angel *n.* (d) Amytal. See AMYTAL; BARBITURATE.

blue balls *n.* Pain in the testicles due to extreme sexual excitement without release through ejaculation. **a.k.a.** love nuts.

blue barrel *n.* (d) Barrel-shaped tablet, blue in color, that contains LSD.

blue bird *n.* (d) Amytal sodium capsule. Name comes from color of capsule.

blue boy. See POLICEMAN.

blue cheer *n.* (d) Type of LSD usually mixed with Methedrine. See LYSERGIC ACID DIETHYLAMIDE; METHEDRINE.

blue dot *n.* Usually a white tablet with a drop of blue liquid LSD on it.

blue heaven *n.* (d) Amytal. See AMYTAL; BARBITURATE.

blue velvet *n.* (d) Paregoric (camphorated tincture of opium) and Pyribenzamine (an antihistamine) mixed and injected.

bluejeans *n.* (d) Particular type of LSD from New York, not available on the West Coast. Very blue in color, from which the name comes. See HALLUCINOGEN; LYSERGIC ACID DIETHYLAMIDE.

blues *n.* Feeling of depression—eg. *I have the blues.*

blunt *n.* (p) Knife.

B.M.O.C. Big man on campus; refers to very popular, important individual on a college campus.

body drug *n.* (d) Physically addictive drug such as heroin; to be differentiated from a head drug, such as a hallucinogen.

bogart (bō'-gahrt) *v.* **1.** (d) Take longer than necessary to pass a marijuana cigarette—eg. *Don't bogart that joint.* Comes from the manner in which actor Humphrey Bogart smoked a cigarette. **2.** Hog.

bogue *adj.* (d) In need of narcotics; suffering from a need for narcotics; experiencing withdrawal symptoms.

bogus *adj.* Phony; unreal; fake—eg. *What did you do with the bogus money?*

bolsa (bōl'-sah) *n.* (d) Bag; small packet of narcotics. Comes from Spanish *bolsa,* meaning pouch or bag. See BAG.

bombed out *adj.* (d) Totally under the influence of a drug; very high.

bomber *n.* (d) Very large rolled marijuana cigarette. See MARIJUANA CIGARETTE.

bombita *n.* (d) Methedrine. See AMPHETAMINE; METHEDRINE.

bombito *n.* (d) Vial of Desoxyn.

bon-a-roo (bahn'-a-roo) *adj.* (m) Fantastic; the ultimate of all being—eg. *The bike pack to San Francisco was bon-a-roo!* See GROOVY.

boncha (*Spanish* bɔn-chə) *n.* Bunch; members of a gang.

bone *n.* **1.** The middle finger put up alone, a gesture that means fuck you—eg. *He flipped me the bone.* **a.k.a.** bird. See FUCK; FUCK YOU. **2.** Penis See PENIS.

boner *n.* **1.** An erection. **2.** Error; mistake—eg. *That was a real boner!*

boo *n.* Marijuana. See MARIJUANA.

boob *n.* **1.** Black person. Originated in New York; derogatory. **2.** Female's breast. See BREAST. **3.** Dumb person; person without understanding.

book *n.* Telephone book kept by a prostitute, consisting of phone numbers, addresses and descriptions of clients. It is sold for very high sums of money when a prostitute leaves the business or changes her location.

book, the *n. Physicians' Desk Reference,* considered the drug addicts' bible although its original purpose was for classification and description of medication for physicians' use. **a.k.a.** P.D.R. See *PHYSICIANS' DESK REFERENCE.*

boost *v.* **1.** (d, pr) Prostitute oneself (a female) for money to buy narcotics. **2.** (d) Steal merchandise to sell for money to buy narcotics. **3.** Steal; shoplift—eg. *I boosted the store for a sweater and got five dollars for it.* **4.** Get rid of stolen goods.

booster pill *n.* (d) Amphetamine; an upper. See AMPHETAMINE.

boot *v.* (d) Inject a drug intravenously a little at a time, letting it back up in the eyedropper, then injecting a little more, letting the blood-and-drug mixture back up and so on. **a.k.a.** jack, jerk off. *n.* An injection of a narcotic. See INJECTION.

booze *n.* Alcoholic beverage.

bopper *n.* Hip, aware young person in tune with the modern scene. Used with another word or a prefix to distinguish age—eg. *maxibopper, microbopper, minibopper, teenybopper.*

border *n.* Low-potency Seconal pill; a downer. Called border because it comes from south of the border (Mexico). See BARBITURATE; SECONAL.

borracho (*Spanish* bo-rah′-chō) *n.* A drunk. *adj.* Drunk.

boss *adj.* Great; fantastic; groovy. See GROOVY.

B.O.T. *n.* (p) Balance of time. When a person violates his parole and is returned to prison, he must serve out the balance remaining from his original sentence.

bouncing powder *n.* (d) Cocaine. See COCAINE.

box *n.* Vagina. See VAGINA.

boxed *adj.* **1.** (d) Intoxicated on a drug; high. See LOADED. **2.** (p) In jail.

boy *n.* (d) Heroin. See HEROIN.

boy scout *n.* See POLICEMAN.

B.R. *n.* money, from the first two letters of the word bread, which means money. See MONEY.

brain tickler *n.* (d) Pill.

bread *n.* Money. See MONEY.

breast *n.* **a.k.a.** bazoom, big brown eye, boob, can, chestnut, globe, jug, knocker, marshmallow, ninny jug, tit.

breath freshener *n.* Substance to sweeten the breath; sniffed to obtain a high.

brick *n.* (d) **1.** Pound or 2.2 pounds (a kilo) of marijuana tightly compressed. When in one-pound bricks, it can be shipped in candy boxes. **a.k.a.** bar. **2.** Hashish can also be obtained in brick form, but it is not the same quantity as marijuana. **a.k.a.** bar, block.

bring down *v.* Depress someone following an elated feeling that can be, but is not necessarily, from the effect of drugs. *n.* **1.** Any thing or action that depresses one. **2.** Statement that causes a deflation of another's mood. **3.** Insult; remark that puts someone in his place—eg. *That was a real bring down.*

broad *n.* Casual term for a female. See FEMALE.

brocas (*Spanish* brō'-kahs) Bucks; money. See MONEY.

brother *n.* (B) Term used by a Black man or woman to identify a Black male and as a term of address. See SISTER.

Brown *adj.* Mexican-American; Mexican.

Brown Berets *n.* Pro-Mexican-American militant organization, similar to the Black Panther organization. See BLACK PANTHERS.

brown boy *n.* One who obtains sexual gratification by ingesting fecal matter, ie., eating shit (medically known as coprophilia). **a.k.a.** fecal freak. See DINGLE BERRY.

brown job *n.* Oral copulation of the anus. **a.k.a.** ream job, rim job. See DINGLE BERRY; REAM JOB.

brown nose *v.* Fawn over someone; get in good with someone. Comes from getting one's nose brown with fecal matter from "kissing someone's ass." **a.k.a.** kiss someone's ass. See ASS KISSER; KISSY.

brown stuff *n.* Heroin from Mexico. Name comes from the color, as differentiated from white stuff. See HEROIN.

brownie *n.* Brownie made with marijuana baked in it. The effect from eating such a brownie is like smoking marijuana. Marijuana is also cooked in fudge, spaghetti and other things. See ALICE B. TOKLAS.

brush *n.* **1.** Mustache. **2.** Female's pubic area. **a.k.a.** bush.

brutal *adj.* Very bad; negative; physically or psychologically hurting.

B.S. *n.* Bullshit. See BULLSHIT.

B.S.U. *n.* Black Student Union. An organization on high-school and college campuses composed of

Black students. Its purpose is to promote the welfare of Black students and the study of Black culture in the U.S. and relevant issues. Some affiliates of the national organization are militant.

bubble gum *adj.* Describes anything that appeals to young adolescents (teenyboppers), usually considered by older people to be of silly or shallow composition—eg. *They like bubble gum music.* See TEENYBOPPER.

buck *n.* **1.** Virile young Black male. Term used by whites and considered derogatory by Blacks. **2.** Dollar.

Buddahead *n.* Oriental person.

budgy *adj.* (B) Fat.

bug *v.* Bother; annoy—eg. *That girl can bug me more than anyone else.*

buggy *adj.* **1.** Crazy. **2.** Extremely neurotic; in a state of extreme anxiety.

buggy, horse and See HORSE AND BUGGY.

bulb *n.* (d) Inner core of a capsule, eg., Darvon, the pain killer, is a small round ball (bulb) surrounded by powdered Bufferin.

bull *n.* **1.** Talk that amounts to very little; small talk; talk that is untrue—eg. *We shot the bull for a while.* **a.k.a.** bullshit, garbage, jive. **2.** (p) Policeman; prison guard. See POLICEMAN.

bull dyke *n.* Lesbian who plays a masculine role, dresses in male clothes and assumes male postures and attitudes. See BUTCH; LESBIAN.

bull horrors *n.* (d) Aftereffects of using cocaine.

bullet *n.* **1.** (p) One-year term in prison. **2.** (B) One dollar.

bullshit *v.* Talk; make small talk; talk verbosely, exaggeratedly. **a.k.a.** shuck. *n.* Talk that amounts to very little; small talk; talk without meaning; talk that is untrue. **a.k.a.** bull, garbage, jive, shuck.

bum *v.* Obtain something for free; beg—eg. *Can I bum a cigarette from you?*

bum bend *n.* (d) Frightening and/or depressing experience, usually when under the influence of LSD (or any drug). **a.k.a.** bad trip, bum kicks, bum trip, down trip.

bum kicks *n.* (d) Frightening and/or depressing experience, usually when under the influence of LSD (or any drug). **a.k.a.** bad trip, bum bend, bum trip, down trip.

bum rap *n.* (p) Suspicion, arrest or conviction for a crime of which one is not guilty.

bum trip *n.* (d) Frightening and/or depressing experience, usually when under the influence of LSD (or any drug). **a.k.a.** bad trip, bum bend, bum kicks, down trip.

bummer *n.* Unpleasant, disappointing or negative experience—eg. *That show was a bummer* or *I lost my job; what a bummer!*

bump heads *v.* Fight.

bundle *n.* **1.** Small package of narcotics, usually heroin, morphine or cocaine. See BAG. **2.** Package of a number of bags of heroin tied together in a bundle, usually bought by a dealer to resell them.

bunny *n.* Sexually uninhibited female.

bunny fuck *v.* **1.** Engage in sexual intercourse that occurs quickly. **2.** Procrastinate; waste time and accomplish nothing—eg. *Quit bunny fucking around.*

buns *n.* buttocks.

burn *v.* **1.** Steal. **2.** (d) Accept money and give no drug in return—eg. *He burned me.* **3.** (d) Inform on someone for drug activity. **4.** Hurt emotionally. **a.k.a.** do in.

burn artist *n.* **1.** (d) Drug seller who sells with the intent not to deliver. **2.** (p) Police informer.

burn coal *v.* Date a Black person.

burned out *adj.* **1.** (d) Sclerotic, very punctured condition of a vein, present in most addicts; means the vein cannot be used or is difficult to use for injection. See CRATER. **2.** (d) Having reached the stage where the drug one is taking fails to provide further satisfaction or the desired effect. **3.** Condition resulting from overuse—eg. *I wanted to make love a third time, but I was burned out.*

burnt See BURN.
bush *n.* **1.** (d) Marijuana. See MARIJUANA. **2.** Female. See FEMALE. **3.** Pubic hair. **a.k.a.** beaver, brush, furburger, hairburger, hairpie. **4.** Mustache. **a.k.a.** brush. **5.** New hairdo.
business *n.* (d) Equipment used for preparing and injecting drugs. See FIT.
businessman's trip *n.* Experience after smoking or injecting dimethyltryptamine (DMT), a hallucinogen. So named because the effects last only one-half to one hour and it can be taken on a lunch hour. See DIMETHYLTRYPTAMINE; HALLUCINOGEN.
bust *v.* **1.** Arrest. **2.** Catch someone doing something he shouldn't be doing. **3.** Hit (physically). **4.** Confront. **5.** Inform on. *n.* **1.** Police raid. **2.** Situation that turns out to be unpleasant—eg. *My home life is a bust.*
bust a cap *v.* (d) Take a narcotic.
busted *adj.* **1.** Arrested; caught. **2.** Confronted. **3.** Squealed on; informed on.
busted but not twisted *adj.* (p) Arrested but not convicted. See HUMMER.
butch *n.* Lesbian who plays the male role. See BULL DYKE, LESBIAN.
button *n.* Round top of the peyote cactus plant. **a.k.a.** top. See HALLUCINOGEN; PEYOTE.
buttons, press someone's See PRESS SOMEONE'S BUTTONS.
buy off *v.* **1.** Bribe someone, usually a guard in prison. **2.** Avoid a task; shirk a duty or obligation.
buy the dick *v.* **1.** Get into trouble; get hurt. **2.** Die—eg. *He bought the dick through an overdose.*
buy the farm *v.* Die.
buzz *v.* Try to buy drugs. *n.* Feeling of being high or

lightheaded, caused by drugs or alcohol--eg. *I feel a buzz.*

B.Y.O.B. Bring your own bottle *or* Bring your own booze. Used with verbal or written invitations to parties. See BOOZE.

C

C *n.* (d) Cocaine. See COCAINE.

C and H *n.* (d) Mixture of cocaine and heroin. **a.k.a.** cold and hot.

C and M *n.* (d) Mixture of cocaine and morphine.

caballo (*Spanish* kah-bah'-lyō) *n.* Horse; translation of the American term for heroin.

cabrón (*Spanish* kah-brōn') *n.* Bastard.

ca-ca (kah-kah) *n.* Puerto Rican and Mexican slang for shit; used as a translation of the American term for heroin or marijuana.

cactus *n.* **1.** Money. See MONEY. **2.** Mescaline. See HALLUCINOGEN; MESCALINE.

cadet *n.* (d) Novice user of heroin.

cage *n.* School.

cal de aquellos (*Spanish* kahl' dā ah ke'-lyōs) Expression meaning fine, great, groovy.

calabuso (*Spanish* kah-lah-bōō'-sō) *n.* Jail. See CLINK.

call *v.* Confront another person. **a.k.a.** call someone on something.

call someone on something See CALL.

calling card *n.* **1.** (d) Needle mark, or track, made by injection of drugs into the veins that acts as proof to other addicts that one is not a narcotics or undercover agent, but an addict. See TRACK. **2.** Description of a prostitute's client.

calo (*Spanish* kah'-lō) *n.* Penny. **a.k.a.** clemo, fierro.

camp *v.* (h) Present oneself in voice, gesture, words and dress effeminately in order to let another homosexual know one is a homosexual and interested in relations; flirt—eg. *They were camping.* *adj.* **1.** Describes the taking of old, accepted, sacred standards and symbols of the Establishment and ridiculing them and their sacredness by using them in once-unaccepted and unorthodox situations, also implying that values are not constant or absolute, eg., the American flag in clothing and interior decor. **2.** Applied to old-style art, clothing and other objects recently considered very old-fashioned and out of style that are in vogue again because of their oldness.

can *n.* **1.** (d) One ounce of marijuana. **a.k.a.** lid. See QUANTITIES OF DRUGS. **2.** (p) Jail; prison; police station. See CLINK. **3.** Rest room. **a.k.a.** john. **4.** Woman's breast. See BREAST. **5.** Opium. See OPIUM. **6.** Car. See CAR.

can of opium *n.* (d) Unit of measurement usually 2 1/2 or 5 inches tall, weighing 3 1/2 or 6 2/3 ounces respectively.

Canadian black *n.* (d) Marijuana grown in Canada. See MARIJUANA.

Canadian bouncer *n.* (d) Form of inferior-quality Seconal from Canada. See BARBITURATE; SECONAL.

candy *n.* (d) Drugs.

candy man *n.* (d) Seller of drugs. See PUSHER.

Cannabis sativa *n.* (med) Botanical name for marijuana. The intoxicating element comes from the amber-colored resin of the flowering tops and leaves of the female hemp plant. See MARIJUANA.

canton (*Spanish* kahn-tōn') *n.* Home.

cap *n.* **1.** Drug in capsule form. **2.** Empty capsule to be filled with a drug.

cap on *v.* Look at—eg. *You sure capped on that girl.*

car *n.* **a.k.a.** can, dubee, duby, hog, sheen, short, wheels.

Carbona *n.* (d) Brand of cleaning fluid. Its fumes are inhaled for their intoxicating effect.

carga (*Spanish* kahr'-gah) *n.* Bundle of marijuana.

cargador (*Spanish* kahr-gah-dor') *n.* Carrier of marijuana.

carnal (*Spanish* kahr-nahl') *n.* Good friend; brother. **a.k.a.** mano.

carpet walker *n.* (d) Confirmed addict. **a.k.a** lifer.

carruchar (*Spanish* kahr-rōō-chahr') *v.* Arrest or pick up for questioning.

carry *v.* (d) Be in possession of a drug. **a.k.a.** hold.

cartoon *v.* (d) Having a visual experience—eg. *I'm cartooning.* *n.* (d) Hallucination; visual experience caused usually by the use of drugs. **a.k.a.** pattern, trail.

cartwheel *n.* (d) **1.** Dexamyl. See AMPHETAMINE; BARBITURATE; DEXAMYL. **2.** Dexedrine. See AMPHETAMINE; DEXEDRINE.

case *v.* (p) To look over a place—eg. *Case the joint.* *n.* **1.** One's story or tale. **2.** Personal problem—eg. *What's your case?* **3.** Being attracted to someone; a crush—eg. *I've got a case for him.*

case, on the See ON THE CASE.

casual *adj.* Attractive; all right—eg. *That book was really casual.*

cat *n.* **1.** Man who dresses in the latest style. **2.** Any man—eg. *Who's that cat across the street?* **3.** Vicious, gossiping woman. **4.** (d) Supplier of drugs.

catch *n.* (h, p) Recipient in a homosexual relationship; the receiver of anal intercourse or oral copulation; the female part of the homosexual relationship. Common usage in prison. See PITCH.

catch someone up *v.* Catch someone in a lie or an untruth—eg. *He caught me up.*

catnip *n.* (d) Stimulant for cats. Smoked with marijuana to obtain a high; also used to cut (water down) marijuana to sell less for the money.

cent *n.* (d) One dollar. See DIME BAG; NICKEL BAG.

chale (*Spanish* chah'-lā) No—eg. *Do you want some candy? Chale.* **a.k.a.** nel.

chalk *n.* (d) Amphetamine. Comes from white color and chalky consistency. See AMPHETAMINE.

champ *n.* (d) Addict who won't inform to police no matter how sick he is. Sometimes the police say they will give a fix (drug injection) to the person who is withdrawing in exchange for information.

changes *n.* **1.** State of anxiety or tension due to attitude changes of the individual. See GO THROUGH CHANGES. **2.** Realization of a fact and the changes in one's attitudes or behavior with this realization. See GO THROUGH CHANGES; PUT SOMEONE THROUGH CHANGES. **3.** (d) Attitude changes a person goes through while on drugs.

charas *n.* (d) Marijuana. From a Hindi word. See MARIJUANA.

charge *n.* **1.** (d) Effects from a drug. **2.** Marijuana. See MARIJUANA. **3.** Kicks; thrills; excitement— eg. *Get a charge* = *Get kicks*.

charged up *adj.* (d) Under the effect of narcotics.

Charlie *n.* **1.** White man. See MISTER CHARLIE. **2.** (d) Cocaine. See COCAINE. **3.** One dollar; five Charlies = five dollars.

check out *v.* **1.** See what is happening to someone, something or at some place—eg. *Let's check out the party*. **a.k.a.** scope out. **2.** find out about; look into. **a.k.a.** scope out.

cherry *n.* **1.** Hymen—eg. *He broke her cherry*. **2.** Male or female virgin. **3.** Any person who has never done something; a novice.

cherry kicks *n.* (d) Initial injection of drugs after an addict's release from prison. See CHERRY.

chestnut *n.* Female's breast. See BREAST.

chestnuts *n.* Testicles. See TESTICLES.

chew five-day deodorant pads (d) A way to get high, common among 8th, 9th and 10th graders.

Chicago black *n.* (d) Black marijuana. See MARIJUANA.

Chicago green *n.* (d) Form of marijuana that is grown in Chicago and is dark green in color. **a.k.a.** Illinois green. See MARIJUANA.

chicano (*Spanish* chē-kah'-nō) *n.* Mexican-American or Mexican.

chick *n.* Female, usually, but not necessarily, attractive, pert and lively. See FEMALE.

chicken *n.* **1.** Person who is scared, cowardly or afraid —eg. *He's chicken*. **2.** Young homosexual. *adj.* Scared; cowardly; afraid.

chicken out *v.* Fail to fulfill a commitment because of being afraid of consequences—eg. *He said he would tell her, but he chickened out.*

chicken shit *adj.* Usually refers to behavior or a deed as the lowest or most despicable act—eg. *I told him that hitting a child was chicken shit.*

chief, the *n.* (d) **1.** LSD. See HALLUCINOGEN; LYSERGIC ACID DIETHYLAMIDE. **2.** Mescaline. See HALLUCINOGEN; MESCALINE.

chill *v.* **1.** Give a cold shoulder to someone; ignore. **2.** (d) Refuse to sell drugs to someone.

china white *n.* Heroin when it is white in color. See HEROIN.

Chinese tobacco *n.* (d) Opium. See OPIUM.

chingado (*Spanish* chin-gah'-dō) *n.* mother fucker. See MOTHER FUCKER.

chip *v.* (d) **1.** Cheat, in the sense of saying you are not using drugs but really are—eg. *He's been chipping.* **2.** Use drugs only occasionally. **a.k.a.** dabble. See JOY POP.

chip clipper *n.* Female who frequents Nevada casinos. She flirts with men who are gambling to get them to place bets for her. Some make their living this way.

chippy *n.* **1.** (d) Person who occasionally uses drugs while pretending not to. **2.** one who uses drugs only occasionally. **a.k.a.** dabbler, joy rider. See JOY POPPER. **3.** Person who cheats at anything.

chiquita (*Spanish* chē-kē'-tah) *n.* A little taste of drugs. Word translates as "small."

chiva (*Spanish* chē'-vah) *n.* Heroin. See HEROIN.

chloral hydrate *n.* (med) Non-barbiturate sedative. An overdose can cause an effect similar to barbiturates. When used in excess it is called knockout drops. **a.k.a.** joy juice, Mickey Finn, peter.

chlorpromazine hydrochloride (klor-prom'-ə-zēn hī-drə-klor'-īd) *n.* (med) Substance commonly used by drug takers, specifically LSD users, to reduce hallucinations and panic. It is medically used for the control of agitation, anxiety, tension, confusion, and related symptoms in nervous and psychotic conditions, as well as severe personality disorders. See THORAZINE.

cholo (*Spanish* chō'-lō) *n.* **1.** pachuco. See PACHUCO. **2.** Term used by whites meaning a Mexican. **3.** Person of mixed blood, commonly used in Mexican-American community.

choogle *v.* (B) Progress; continue what has been started. Became popular through the lyrics of a song by a group named Creedence Clearwater Revival—eg. *Choogle on* or *Choogle down the highway.*

chop *v.* Insult someone with a remark, a dig or a criticism—eg. *I'm going to chop you so low, you'll have to look up to tie your shoelaces.* **a.k.a.** chop down. *n.* an insult. **a.k.a.** chop down, cut, dig.

chop down See CHOP.

chopped-hog *n.* (m) Modified Harley-Davidson motorcycle, stripped of all chrome. Usually a used police motorcycle. Hog refers to a Harley-Davidson motorcycle, which is very large and fast.

chopper *n.* **1.** (m) Modified motorcycle, stripped of all chrome. **2.** Machine gun or any fast repeating gun.

chota (*Spanish* chō'-tah) *n.* Police; cops. **a.k.a.** azules, tombos. See POLICEMAN.

chow down *v.* Eat. **a.k.a.** scarf, tank up.

Christmas tree *n.* (d) Tuinal; a downer. Comes from its red-and-green coloring. See BARBITURATE; TUINAL.

chucks, the *n.* (d) Intense craving for food, usually sweets. This occurs generally about a week after a person has withdrawn from an addictive drug, usually heroin. **a.k.a.** long cut.

chunks *n.* (d) Hashish. See HASHISH.

circle jerk *n.* Men in a circle engaged in mutual masturbation. Done with each individual masturbating another or with each individual masturbating himself, often in a contest to see who ejaculates first or farthest. See DAISY CHAIN.

C.K. (*Spanish* sā'kah') *n.* Cocaine. See COCAINE.

clap *n.* Venereal disease, usually gonorrhea.

clarabelle *n.* (d) Tetrahydrocannabinol; THC. **a.k.a.** clay, synthetic grass. See TETRAHYDROCANNABINOL.

Class A narcotics *n.* Federal Bureau of Narcotics category of addictive narcotics; opium and its derivatives. Used with regard to the prescription and manufacture of such drugs.

Class B narcotics *n.* Federal Bureau of Narcotics category of drugs that are almost non-addictive, eg., nalline, codeine.

Class M narcotics *n.* Federal Bureau of Narcotics category of non-addictive drugs.

Class X narcotics *n.* Federal Bureau of Narcotics category of drugs containing very small amounts of narcotics combined with non-narcotic medications, eg., codeine cough syrup.

clay *n.* (d) Tetrahydrocannabinol; THC. **a.k.a.** clarabelle, synthetic grass. See TETRAHYDROCANNABINOL.

clean *adj.* **1.** Not using drugs. **2.** Not in possession of drugs. **3.** Describes marijuana devoid of twigs, stems and seeds, ie., only the best part, the leaves. See DIRTY; MANICURE.

cleaning fluids *n.* Various products inhaled to obtain a high. They provide initial exhilaration and excitement; other reactions are uncoordinated actions, double vision, slurred pronunciation and a buzzing sensation in the ears. They can cause liver, kidney and bone-marrow damage. Brain and chromosome damage has also been reported.

clear up *v.* (d) Stop using an addictive drug. **a.k.a.** take a cure, withdraw.

clemo (*Spanish* kle'-mō). *n.* Penny. **a.k.a.** calo, fierro.

clink *n.* Jail; prison cell. **a.k.a.** calabuso, can, hotel, house, pinta, slams, tilde.

clip *n.* (d) Holder for a marijuana cigarette, used when the cigarette has been smoked too far down to hold with bare fingers. Clips can be made from a paper clip, hair clip, match cover folded in half, dental apron clip, etc. More decorative clips can be bought in stores and are sometimes worn as jewelry. They are often made in the shape of peace symbols. **a.k.a.** crutch, jefferson airplane, roach clip.

closet case *n.* (h) One who engages in homosexual activities yet firmly believes he or she is not a homosexual. See CLOSET QUEEN.

closet queen *n.* **1.** Male who dresses in female clothing. Term is commonly used to connote one who indulges only in private, a secret transvestite. **2.** Male who engages in homosexual acts yet firmly believes he is not a homosexual. See CLOSET CASE.

C.O. *n.* Conscientious objector; one who resists induction into military service due to religious or moral belief. Some men choose jail and some go to live in Canada. See RESISTORS.

coast *v.* **1.** Be under the influence of a drug; feel the effects of a drug. **2.** Be in a nodding state. See NOD.

coca (*Spanish*) *n.* Cocaine. See COCAINE.

cocaine *n.* (med) (benzoylmethylecgonine) Strong stimulant in the form of a white powder that is swallowed, injected or sniffed. It has a euphoric and exhilarating effect; not physically addictive but can cause marked psychic dependence. Chronic use produces hallucinations and paranoia, then depression; severe depression upon withdrawal sometimes leads to suicide. Sniffing cocaine may cause perforation of the nasal septum and brain damage. It was medically used as a local anesthetic before the advent of modern drugs. Long-time users may suffer from malnutrition and anemia due to curtailed appetite. The drug appeals especially to psychopathic individuals who are likely to commit serious antisocial acts. **a.k.a.** Bernice, big bloke, bouncing powder, C, Charlie, C.K., coca, coke, corrine, cubes, flake,

girl, gold dust, happy dust, her, the leaf, sea, snow, star dust, white drugs, white stuff.
cochino (*Spanish* kō-chē'-nō) *n.* Pig. *adj.* Dirty.
cock *n.* Penis. See PENIS.
cock bite *n.* Disagreeable female; bitch.
cock-sucker *n.* **1.** One who engages in oral intercourse. Comes from cock, which means penis. See ORAL COPULATION. **2.** Insult; oblique inference to the status of one's masculinity.
cocktail n. (d) End portion of a marijuana cigarette put into the top of a regular cigarette and smoked. See ROACH; SEED.
codeine *n.* (med) (methylmorphine) Drug that is derived from morphine. Codeine can be swallowed or injected. Duration of action is usually four hours. It is medically used as a local anesthetic and also in the treatment of severe cough. Commonly used by heroin addicts between heroin injections to "tide them over." **a.k.a.** cubes, school boy.
codo (*Spanish* kō'-dō) *adj.* **1.** Having drugs—eg. *Anda codo* means he has drugs. **2.** Stingy.
coil *n.* Intrauterine device; relatively permanent contraceptive. **a.k.a.** I.U.D. See CONTRACEPTIVE.
coins *n.* money. See MONEY.
cojones (*Spanish* kō-hɔ'-nes) *n.* **1.** Balls; testicles. See TESTICLES. **2.** Courage—eg. *Tiene cojones* = *He's got balls (courage).* **a.k.a.** balls, hair, juice.
coke *n.* (d) Cocaine. See COCAINE.
coke head *n.* (d) Cocaine addict. See HEAD.
coked up *adj.* (d) Under the influence of cocaine.
cokie (kō'-kē). *n.* Cocaine addict.
cold *adj.* Bad; unfeeling; insensitive; raw (deal)—eg. *He's cold* or *That's really cold, man.*
cold and hot *n.* (d) Mixture of cocaine and heroin. **a.k.a.** C and H.
cold cock *v.* **1.** Knock out someone with fists. **2.** Hit someone mentally, leaving him with no comeback.

cold shot *n.* **1.** Verbal insult; put-down. **2.** Act that would bring dissension.

cold turkey *adv.* (d) Withdrawing from drugs without the aid of any medication—eg. *He went off heroin cold turkey.* See ON THE NATCH; WITHDRAWAL.

collar *n.* Piece of string or paper or dollar bill put tightly around an eyedropper between the dropper and the needle or between the bulb and the dropper when injecting a drug to seal it off from the air to create better suction.

colorado (*Spanish* kō-lō-rah′-dō) *n.* Red; Seconal. **a.k.a.** rojito. See BARBITURATE; SECONAL.

colors *n.* People of any race or ethnic origin. Commonly used by flower children—eg. *He walks with all colors.* See FLOWER CHILDREN.

come *v.* Climax (male and female); ejaculate. **a.k.a.** cream, cum, get one's nuts off. *n.* Semen. **a.k.a.** cum, jissom, load.

come down *v.* **1.** (d) Lose the drug-induced exhilaration as the drug wears off. **a.k.a.** re-enter. **2.** Change of emotional levels from a higher (happier) level to a lower (sadder or depressed) one.

come down on *v.* Tell off; bawl out; act verbally punitive.

come on *v.* **1.** (d) Begin to experience the effects of a drug. **2.** Flirt; make sexual advances toward either sex. *n.* A line; act of enticing someone to spend money. See CON; CON GAME.

commune *n.* **1.** Community where nothing is privately owned, where all goods and responsibilities are commonly owned and shared. The residents are usually permanent. **2.** House or living premises shared by many people (male and female). The usual established social and sexual mores are negligible. Money is shared by all residents. This type of commune is often associated with hippies. **3.** Large house shared by many people, each contributing equally. These exist and are becoming more popular in college communities. The duration of residency often coincides with the semester or quarter system of the college.

compadre (*Spanish* kom-pah'-drā) *n.* Pal; old friend. **a.k.a.** cuate.

Compazine *n.* (med) (Smith, Kline & French Laboratories) Major tranquilizer.

con *v.* Cheat; steal; manipulate people out of their money. Comes from confidence game. **a.k.a.** hit on someone, shuck, snow job. See CON GAME; HUSTLE; HYPE; WORK (SOMEONE). *n.* **1.** Ex-convict. **a.k.a.** shuck. **2.** Homosexual. See HOMOSEXUAL.

con game *n.* Line, lie, trick used to manipulate a person or group of people or institution (usually for profit). Comes from confidence games. An example of a con game is the Murphy game in which a man approaches another man who is looking for a prostitute, gains his confidence by talking, takes his money and leaves, promising to have a female return when in reality there is no female. **a.k.a.** flim-flam, hype. See HUSTLER.

con safos (*Spanish* kon sah'-fōs) Expression meaning **1.** I'm impervious to your attacks or **2.** The same to you. It is written C/S on walls where one writes one's own name or gang name, meaning anything said about one or one's gang will "bounce off and stick to the attacker."

conductor on the trolley *n.* (d) Narcotics runner along the organized channels of distribution. He takes the drug from the dealer (seller) and makes deliveries; he also cuts the drug and sells it for his own profit. See CUT.

confront *v.* Bring to one's attention, in a very overt fashion, an aspect concerning him, usually something that is not complimentary.

Congo mataby *n.* African term for marijuana. See MARIJUANA.

connect *v.* (d) Purchase drugs.

connection *n.* (d) Drug dealer or intermediary; source of drugs; anyone who sells drugs is a connection

contact to whoever buys from him. **a.k.a.** swingman. See CONDUCTOR ON THE TROLLEY; CONTACT.

contact *n.* (d) **1.** Seller of drugs. **2.** Go-between between the drug user and the dealer (seller). See CONDUCTOR ON THE TROLLEY; CONNECTION.

contact habit *n.* (d) Vicarious drug habit, ie., the clothes, style of living, language, friends, moods and attitudes of a drug addict, though not oneself using drugs. Comes from constant contact with addicts, pushers, narcotics agents.

contact high *n.* (d) **1.** A high induced by merely being in the presence of others who are under the influence of a drug, induced because of the exposure and not by the physical state of taking a drug. **2.** A high that is derived from breathing the smoke that accumulates from other people who are smoking marijuana.

contraceptive *n.* Birth control device. Among them are the coil, other intrauterine devices, the pill, foam, prophylactics. See your doctor.

cook *v.* **1.** (d) Heat a powdered drug or a pill with water to obtain a solution that can be injected. **a.k.a.** cook up, pan up. See FIT; SUPPLIES. **2.** Get going; be intensely involved in what one is doing —eg. *Cook, baby, cook!* **3.** (mu) Improvise well, usually during jazz solos and usually oblivious to all but the music itself. Also implies excitement in a musician's performance—eg. *He's really cooking now.*

cook me down Expression said when you want to have sexual intercourse with someone; a request.

cook up *v.* Heat any powdered form of drug with water to liquefy it for injection. **a.k.a.** cook, pan up.

cooker *n.* Spoon or bottle cap used in the preparation of a powdered drug in order to be able to inject it. The powdered drug is placed in the cooker with a few drops of water, heated over an open flame (often a match or lighter) and stirred until it dissolves into solution; then cotton is placed in the solution to draw it up and any form of syringe is used to pull the drug from the cotton (see COTTON). When a spoon is used, the handle is bent in the middle for easier holding and also to concentrate the heat in the bowl of the spoon.

cool *adj.* **1.** Self-assured; knowledgeable; aware of the times. Term is becoming obsolete in favor of "in." **2.** Satisfying; pleasant; attractive. **3.** Describes a person who never loses control of his temper. **4.** Applied to a style of jazz usually associated with improvisations and soft tones. This type of jazz resembles classical music, as evidenced by the music of jazz cellist Fred Katz, who through his own playing, writing and teaching has innovated and furthered this art form.

cool head *n.* **1.** (d) Person who is able to take drugs and not have his behavior or attitudes visibly change. **2.** Someone whom you admire. **3.** Someone who is self-assured. See COOL.

cool it *v.* **1.** Stop. **2.** Stop threatening or being angry; refrain from annoying another person. **3.** Stop or suspend any activity because it may be dangerous or embarrassing. **4.** Calm down; slow down; relax.

cop *v.* **1.** Steal. **2.** (d) Buy or otherwise obtain drugs. **a.k.a.** score. See MAKE. *n.* Policeman. See POLICEMAN.

cop a free feel *v.* Pass someone and without making it appear on purpose, yet doing so intentionally, touch a part of his body. Usually done by a man to a woman.

cop a plea *v.* Plead guilty to a criminal charge, usually in exchange for a light sentence.

cop out *v.* **1.** Avoid a situation. **2.** Find an excuse, usually a phony one, to get out of something or a situation. **3.** Divulge information; admit guilt. **a.k.a.** cop out to, cop to. *n.* Person who cops out.

cop out on *v.* Fail to do something; fail to keep a promise; stand someone up. **a.k.a.** fink out on.

cop out to *v.* Admit something—eg. *He copped out to stealing it.* **a.k.a.** cop out, cop to.

cop to *v.* **1.** Tell or admit something. **a.k.a.** cop out, cop out to. **2.** Plead guilty.

copilot *n.* (d) **1.** Amphetamine; an upper. See AMPHETAMINE. **2.** One who cares for and sits with someone who has taken a drug. See GUIDE.

coprophilia *n.* Act of ingesting fecal matter. See BROWN BOY.

copulate *v.* (med) Have intercourse. **a.k.a.** ball, bang, fuck, get into her pants, get into someone, get it on, hump, jerk, lay, make it, make love, make the scene, nail (someone), nut, pile, punch, ride, rip off, score, screw, shack up (with), shtup, strap, strap on, stroke, trick, work.

copulation *n.* (med) Sexual intercourse. **a.k.a.** big time, hit, leg, nookie, piece, piece of ass, piece of tail, tail, trim.

corn *n.* Hard scar near the vein caused by repeated injections. See TRACK.

corn hole *v.* Engage in anal intercourse, either homosexual or heterosexual. Commonly engaged in by servicemen and prisoners.

corral *n.* (pr) Group of prostitutes who work for a pimp and are known as the pimp's corral.

corrine *n.* Cocaine. See COCAINE.

cotics *n.* (d) Narcotics.

cotton *n.* (d) **1.** Piece of cotton that is placed in the cooker in order to absorb a liquefied drug. The drug is drawn into the syringe through the needle placed in the cotton. These pieces of cotton are saved and the residue is reused by combining a number of pieces and adding water to saturate the cotton to make the residue liquid again. **a.k.a.** satch cotton. See COOKER; POUND COTTON. **2.** Part of inhaler that is saturated with drugs, taken out of inhaler and taken orally.

cotton head *n.* (d) One who adds water to a piece of cotton in order to recook the drug left in it and use it for injection. **a.k.a.** cotton top. See COTTON.

cotton top *n.* (d) One who adds water to a piece of

cotton in order to recook the drug left in it and use it for injection. **a.k.a.** cotton head. See COTTON.

country *adj.* Coming from the country; not versed in city ways; not sophisticated; simple. See WATERMELON HEAD.

coupled *adj.* **1.** In the company of another person, usually of the opposite sex. **2.** Going together; going steady.

coupled off *adj.* With a specific person and only that person—eg. *Everyone was coupled off except me.*

courier *n.* Small-time drug seller.

coyote (*Spanish* kō-yō′-tā) *n.* **1.** Tricky seller of drugs. **2.** Chiseler; swindler.

crab *n.* Small organism that affects pubic hair area and other hairy areas of the body, causing extreme itching and irritation. Communicable by physical contact.

crack *n.* **1.** Female. See FEMALE. **2.** Vagina. See VAGINA.

crack up *v.* **1.** Stop functioning; have a nervous breakdown. **2.** Laugh. **3.** Make one laugh—eg. *She really cracks me up.*

cracker *n.* A white bigot.

crank freak *n.* (d) One who takes different kinds of pills for the purpose of sleeping, waking up, staying up and going to sleep again. Once a person is on this cycle, he feels that he cannot function in society without the pills and so continues using them. This is done by many people who are functional in society.

crank it on *v.* **1.** Go wild; get excited. Usually said when dancing or having a drug or sexual experience. **2.** Lie to someone; tell a wild, exaggerated story.

crap *n.* **1.** Fecal matter. **a.k.a.** dong, shit. **2.** Exclamation of disgust—eg. *Oh, crap!* **3.** (d) Low-quality diluted heroin.

crash *v.* **1.** Pass out; fall asleep. **a.k.a.** fall out, flake out. **2.** Sleep for one or two nights at someone's house. **3.** (d) Lose, gradually or suddenly, the effect of a drug.

crash pad *n.* **1.** Place to sleep, usually for a one-night stay. See ON THE ROAD; SKIPPER; SLEEP ROUGH. **2.** (d) Place to go rest after being high on a drug. **3.** (d) Place where drug users can go to withdraw.

crater *n.* (d) Discolored indentation in the flesh that sometimes results from repeated injections at the same spot. See TRACK.

craw *n.* (B) Throat; sometimes head.

cream *v.* **1.** Ejaculate. **a.k.a.** come, cum, get one's nuts off. **2.** (d) Massage, attempting to make needle tracks disappear.

creep *n.* (d) Addict who begs, does errands or lends out a hypodermic needle in exchange for a taste of someone else's drugs.

cresta (*Spanish* kres'-tah) *n.* LSD. See HALLUCINOGEN; LYSERGIC ACID DIETHYLAMIDE. **a.k.a.** cresto.

cresto (*Spanish* kres'-tō). See CRESTA.

crib *n.* Place of dwelling. See HOME.

croaker *n.* (d, p) Unethical doctor who, for a high fee, will prescribe a drug. Croaker is the prison term for doctor. Comes from croak, which means die. **a.k.a.** hungry croaker.

crowded *adj.* Badgered or verbally set upon by another; having no verbal response or escape— eg. *I don't like being crowded.*

crow's nest *n.* Home, a house or apartment. See HOME.

cruise *v.* **1.** Look for excitement. **2.** Ride around in your car with either no specific objective or looking for sexual companionship, homosexual or heterosexual. **3.** Get along o.k.; function without difficulty.

crutch *n.* (d) **1.** Device used to hold a roach, or butt of a marijuana cigarette, to enable one to smoke it completely without burning the fingers. **a.k.a.** clip, jefferson airplane, roach clip. **2.** Container for a hypodermic.

crystal *n.* (d) Drug in powder form, often Methedrine.

crystal ship *n.* (d) Syringe that contains a crystalline drug, usually heroin or Methedrine.

crystallize *v.* When a powdered drug, usually a barbiturate, not thoroughly in solution, is injected, the crystals of the drug will cause a painful lump that lasts for some time.

C.T. *n.* (B) **1.** Colored time. Used in reference to being late. **2.** Cunt teaser. Lesbian term for a female who acts as if she wants to engage in lesbian sexual activities but won't; heterosexual term for a male who acts desirous of a female in order to be cruel or vicious by exciting her but not having sex with her. **3.** Cock teaser. Female who acts desirous of having sexual intercourse with a male but has no real intention of going through with the act.

cuate (*Spanish* kwah'-tā) *n.* Buddy; pal. **a.k.a.** compadre.

cube *n.* (d) **1.** One gram of hashish. See HASHISH. **2.** Sugar cube that contains LSD. See LSD. **3.** Codeine. See CODEINE.

cubehead *n.* (d) Regular user of LSD sugar cubes. See CUBE.

cubes *n.* (d) **1.** Cocaine. See COCAINE. **2.** Opium. See OPIUM. **3.** Morphine. See MORPHINE. **4.** Codeine. **a.k.a.** school boy. See CODEINE.

cuff *v.* Fail to appear; fail to show up; stand someone up—eg. *He cuffed me again.* **a.k.a.** hang, hang up.

cuffed *adj.* Stood up.

cum See COME.

cunnilingus (kun-ə-ling'-gəs) *n.* (med) Oral-genital copulation by male of female genital area. See FELLATIO; ORAL COPULATION; SPOON; TONGUE.

cunt *n.* **1.** Vagina. See VAGINA. **2.** A female: bitchy, conceited, mean, selfish, malicious, deceiving, cruel, obstinate, disagreeable, bad-tempered. **a.k.a.** bitch. See FEMALE.

cura (*Spanish* kōō'-rah) *n.* **1.** Cure; withdraw from an addictive drug. **2.** Dose of heroin.

curandera (f.) **curandero** (m.) (*Spanish* kur-ahn-de'-rah) *n*. One who deals in home remedies—eg. *curandera de drogas*, one who cures drug users, at home.

curandero (*Spanish* kur-ahn-de'-rō) See CURANDERA.

curbed *adj*. On the curb when hitchhiking. It is illegal to hitchhike from the street.

cure *v*. (d) Artificially hasten the ripening of drugs in plant form by moistening them in a solution of honey or sugar and water or wine or other preparations and letting them dry out.

cure, take a See TAKE A CURE.

cure, the *n*. (d) A sarcastic term used to describe a stay at the U.S. Public Health Service (Narcotics) Hospital at Lexington, Kentucky, in order to withdraw from an addictive drug (usually heroin). Some addicts get arrested and sent to Lexington on purpose when they cannot obtain any drugs because Lexington uses other drugs to take a person off heroin. The most common drug used is methadone, which is very highly addictive. Upon arriving, the addict tells the hospital staff that he is taking double or more the amount he really is because the hospital will cut that amount in half and start to "wean" him with that. Many addicts have said that they never really knew what it meant to be high until they went to Lexington because of the pure drugs used there. Addicts consider Lexington a vacation from the streets. The usual stay is four to six months. The major problem with Lexington is that it deals only with the physical and not the psychological dependence. The program is successful in stopping physical dependence, but its success rate in eliminating psychological dependence is extremely poor, therefore, most addicts who are released from Lexington are physically addicted again in a very short time.

cut *v*. **1.** (d) Decrease potency of a drug by splitting the quantity in half and adding an additional in gredient, usually milk sugar, to the part you are going to sell. This is done to retain some pure drugs for yourself and to increase the quantity sold to make more money. **a.k.a.** sugar down. **2.** Leave. See LEAVE. *n.* Insult. **a.k.a.** chop, chop down, dig.

cut out *v.* Leave; depart. See LEAVE.

cut someone a huss *v.* Do someone a favor.

cyclert *n.* (med) Magnesium hydroxide and permoline; a memory stimulant.

d

dabble *v.* (d) Use narcotics off and on, irregularly. **a.k.a.** chip.

dabbler *n.* (d) One who uses drugs only occasionally. **a.k.a.** chippy.

daddy tank *n.* (p) Prison cell where lesbians are isolated from the rest of the prisoners.

dagga *n.* South African term for marijuana. See MARIJUANA.

daisy chain *n.* Simultaneous sexual activity between three or more people; one person stimulating another who is stimulating another and so on. See CIRCLE JERK; FREAK.

Day-Glo paint *n.* Paint that makes fluorescent materials glow under a black light. It may be used as a body paint. It intensifies colors similar to what is seen during an LSD experience.

deadwood *n.* (d) Government narcotics agent who poses as an addict.

deal *v.* (d) Make a living buying and selling drugs.

dealer *n.* (d) Person who illegally buys and sells drugs for profit. See PUSHER.

debris *n.* (d) Stems and seeds of marijuana left after cleaning it.

deck *n.* (d) Small envelope with about three grains of morphine, heroin or cocaine. See BAG; QUANTITIES OF DRUGS.

deck up *v.* (d) Package a crystallized drug, usually heroin. **a.k.a.** bag.

Demerol *n.* (med) (meperidine hydrochloride; Winthrop Laboratories) A synthetic opiate. It is medically used as an analgesic, or pain reliever. It is physically addictive.

dependence, drug See DRUG DEPENDENCE.

Desbutal *n.* (med) (methamphetamine hydrochloride and pentobarbital sodium; Abbott Laboratories)

A combined amphetamine (Desoxyn) and barbiturate (Nembutal). It is medically used in weight reduction and against depression. The Desoxyn perks one up and the Nembutal keeps one from getting side effects. See AMPHETAMINE; BARBITURATE; DESOXYN; NEMBUTAL.

designs on a person, have See HAVE DESIGNS ON A PERSON.

Desoxyn *n.* (med) (methamphetamine hydrochloride; Abbott Laboratories). Stimulant that directly affects the central nervous system. It is used medically to curtail appetite and relieve depression. See AMPHETAMINE.

destroy *v.* **1.** Confront; smash all defenses. **2.** Put down; insult.

destroyed *adj.* (d) So high on a drug that one cannot move, think or talk well.

DET *n.* (d) Diethyltryptamine. See DIETHYLTRYPTAMINE.

devil *n.* (d) **1.** pill, usually Seconal. Term comes from red color. **2.** STP, a hallucinogen similar to LSD. See HALLUCINOGEN; STP. **3.** Evil white man, a derogatory term.

Dexamyl (dek'-sə-mil) *n.* (med) (Dexedrine and amobarbital; Smith, Kline & French Laboratories) A combined amphetamine and barbiturate. It is medically used to control appetite and relieve depression. **a.k.a.** blue, cartwheel, dexy, purple heart, speedball. See AMPHETAMINE; BARBITURATE.

Dexedrine (dek'-se-drēn) *n.* (med) (dextroamphetamine; Smith, Kline & French Laboratories) Stimulant that affects the central nervous system. It is medically used to control appetite and reduce depression. **a.k.a.** cartwheel, dexy, hi-ball, pep pill. See AMPHETAMINE.

dexy *n.* **1.** Dexamyl. See AMPHETAMINE; BARBITURATE; DEXAMYL. **2.** Dexedrine; an upper. **a.k.a.** cartwheel, heart, rose. See AMPHETAMINE; DEXEDRINE.

dick *n.* Penis. See PENIS.

diethyltryptamine (dī-eth-əl-trip'-tə-mēn) *n.* (d) DET, a quick-acting hallucinogen related to dimethyltryptamine (DMT) and dipropylphyptamine (DPT); a psilocybin-type drug. See DIMETHYLTRYPTAMINE; DIPROPYLPHYPTAMINE; HALLUCINOGEN; PSILOCYBIN.

dig *v.* **1.** Enjoy; appreciate; like; be interested in; be involved in—eg. *I really dig that.* **2.** Question used in a sentence; reference to whether a person is comprehending what is being or has been said—eg. *Are you diggin' it?* See RIGHT. *n.* Insult. **a.k.a.** chop, chop down, cut.

dig it, I can See I CAN DIG IT.

Diggers *n.* A hippy society whose aim is to help hippies. Named after seventeenth-century English farmers who raised food to give to the poor. See HIPPY.

dilated *adj.* Enlarged. Refers to pupils of eyes when under the effect of certain drugs.

Dilaudid (di-lɔ'-did) *n.* (med) (hydromorphone; Knoll Pharmaceutical Company) A semisynthetic derived from morphine. It is used as a pain reliever. Physical dependence develops after prolonged use.

dildo *n.* **1.** Artificial phallus. In olden days it was worn inside the pants to give the appearance of a large penis. Used by lesbians who sexually impersonate males; also used by females for masturbation. See VIBRATOR. **2.** A dumb individual.

dime *n.* (d, pr) Ten dollars.

dime bag *n.* Ten dollars' worth of a crystalline drug. **a.k.a.** 10¢ bag, ten-cent bag. See QUANTITIES OF DRUGS.

dimethyltryptamine (dī-meth-əl-trip'-tə-mēn) *n.* (d) DMT, a hallucinogenic drug related to diethyltryptamine (DET) and dipropylphyptamine (DPT); a psilocybin-type drug. It may be smoked or injected. Its effects are similar to those of LSD but last from only 30 minutes up to four hours. See BUSINESSMAN'S TRIP; DIETHYLTRYPTAMINE; DIPROPYLPHYPTAMINE; HALLUCINOGEN; PSILOCYBIN.

dinghy *n.* mentally unbalanced. **a.k.a.** flaky.

dingle berry *n.* **1.** Lint and fecal matter that gathers and hangs from the pubic hair that surrounds the anus. **2.** Dumb person. **3.** One who ingests dingle berries during sexual play.

dipropylphyptamine *n.* (d) DPT, a hallucinogenic drug related to diethyltryptamine (DET) and dimethyltryptamine (DMT); a psilocybin-type drug. Its effects are similar to those of LSD but last for only an hour or two, and the drug is considered safer than LSD. See BUSINESSMAN'S TRIP; DIETHYLTRYPTAMINE; DIMETHLYTRYPTAMINE; HALLUCINOGEN; PSILOCYBIN.

dirt *n.* (d) Tobacco cigarette. **a.k.a.** hole, square, square joint, straight.

dirt bike *n.* (m) Motorcycle used for mountain or hill riding. **a.k.a.** scrambler.

dirt grass *n.* Uncultivated low-quality marijuana. See MARIJUANA.

dirty *adj.* (d) **1.** Possessing narcotics. **a.k.a.** heeled, holding. **2.** Having taken narcotics. **3.** Refers to marijuana that still contains twigs and seeds. See CLEAN; MANICURE.

discon *n.* (p) Charge or conviction of disorderly conduct.

DMT *n.* (d) Dimethyltryptamine. See DIMETHYLTRYPTAMINE.

do *v.* (h) Suck a penis. See ORAL COPULATION.

do a drug *v.* (d) Use any drug; get stoned, high—eg. *Let's do some grass.*

do bird *v.* (p) Serve a prison sentence. **a.k.a.** do time, serve time.

do for trade *v.* (h) Give someone some action, ie. have sex with someone. See TRADE.

do in *v.* **1.** Insult. **2.** Beat up. **3.** Hurt emotionally. **a.k.a.** burn. **4.** Take advantage of. **5.** Kill (archaic). See THE OLD MOVIES ON TELEVISION.

do right *n.* (d) First-time patient withdrawing from drugs who is considered curable by those giving treatment and by fellow patients.

do right John's *n.* (d) Home of a non-drug-user.

do time *v.* Serve a prison sentence. **a.k.a.** do bird, serve time.

do up *v.* (d) Inject or smoke a drug. Includes all the activities involved in the process of getting high, such as preparing the drug or rolling the cigarette.

do your own thing See DO YOUR THING.

do your thing *v.* Follow your own interests and activities; do whatever you feel is appropriate in your own life, even though this may be in opposition to usual mores and standards; perform activities that are not dependent on those of others or society, but are of your own choice.

D.O.A. Dead on arrival. Officially used by hospitals and police; also employed by drug users.

dogie *n.* (d) Heroin. See HEROIN.

dojee *n.* (d) Heroin. See HEROIN.

dojie *n.* (d) Heroin. See HEROIN.

doll *n.* (d) **1.** Any drug in pill form. Name popularized by book and movie *Valley of the Dolls*. **a.k.a.** dolly. **2.** Seconal. See BARBITURATE; SECONAL.

dolly *n.* (d) **1.** Dolophine. See DOLOPHINE. **2.** Methadone. See METHADONE. **3.** Any drug in pill form. **a.k.a.** doll.

Dolophine (dah'-lō-fen) *n.* (med) (methadone hydrochloride; Eli Lilly and Company) A synthetic opiate used as a substitute for morphine because of its prolonged analgesic effect and action. It is employed in easing withdrawal from heroin. Dolophine is used especially at Lexington (See LEXINGTON) and by psychiatrists in private treatment of patients withdrawing from heroin. **a.k.a.** dolly.

DOM *n.* (d) (2,5-dimethoxy-4-methylamphetamine; Dow Chemical Co.) Hallucinogen similar to LSD and STP. Its effects last a great length of time Large doses may produce disorientation, identity confusion, psychotic reaction and physical trembling. See STP, HALLUCINOGEN.

dome *n.* (d) Type of LSD that derives its name from its domelike shape. See HALLUCINOGEN; LYSERGIC ACID DIETHYLAMIDE.

domino *n.* (d) 12.5-mg. capsule of combined amphetamine and sedative. **a.k.a.** black and white, black and white minstrel, minstrel. See SPEEDBALL.

dong *n.* **1.** Penis. See PENIS. **2.** Fecal matter. **a.k.a.** crap, shit.

don't freeze on me (B) Expression meaning don't leave me out.

don't meth around (d) Expression meaning don't use Methedrine. Sometimes used with Speed kills. See SPEED; SPEED KILLS.

don't sweat it Expression meaning take it easy, don't worry.

don't tread on me Expression meaning (1) don't enforce your values on me, (2) don't force me to do something, (3) don't push me.

doojee *n.* (d) Heroin. See HEROIN.

doojer *n.* (d) Heroin. See HEROIN.

dooji *n.* (d) Heroin. See HEROIN.

doosh bag See DOUCHE BAG.

dope *n.* (d) **1.** Any narcotic or drug. **2.** Term now beginning to apply mainly to marijuana and hallucinogens.

dope fiend *n.* (d) Person who excessively uses any kind of drug. See DOPER; DOPIE; DRUGGIE.

doper *n.* Person who takes drugs and whose attitudes are drug-oriented. **a.k.a.** dopie. See DOPE FIEND; DRUGGIE.

dopie *n.* One who takes drugs. **a.k.a.** doper. See DOPE FIEND; DRUGGIE.

Doriden *n.* (med) (glutethimide; CIBA Pharmaceutical Co.) A non-barbiturate sedative.

dose *n.* **1.** (d) Pills, drugs—eg. *Let's take a dose.* **2.** Prescribed medication. **3.** When used in connection with a venereal disease, implies having a venereal disease—eg. *I've got a dose of clap.* See CLAP.

double trouble *n.* (d) Tuinal. See TUINAL.

douche bag *n.* Obnoxious, sloppy, loud-mouthed person.

dough *n.* money. See MONEY.

down *v.* **1.** Take (swallow) a drug—eg. *The cops came before he downed the pills.* **2.** Criticize negatively. **a.k.a.** put down. *n.* (d) Barbiturate; depressant. **a.k.a.** downer, downie. See BARBITURATE. *adj.* **1.** Unpleasant or depressing. **2.** Depressed. **3.** (d) Off a drug.

down on. See BE DOWN ON; COME DOWN ON; GO DOWN ON.

down trip *n.* Boring, depressing drug experience. **a.k.a.** bad trip, bum bend, bum kicks, bum trip.

downer *n.* (d) **1.** Depressant; barbiturate. Downer is usually used in reference to a sleeping pill. **a.k.a.** down, downie. See BARBITURATE. **2.** Depressing experience.

downie *n.* (d) Barbiturate or tranquilizer pill. **a.k.a.** down, downer. See BARBITURATE.

DPT *n.* (d) Dipropylphyptamine. See DIPROPYLPHYPTAMINE.

drag *n.* Unpleasant, boring person or experience—eg. *He's a drag.* *adv.* With a date—eg. *I'm going drag to the party.* See STAG.

drag, in See IN DRAG.

drag show *n.* (h) performance by female impersonators.

draggin' *v.* Be with a date—eg. *Are you draggin' tonight?*

draw *v.* **1.** (d) Pull blood into the syringe before injecting a drug to verify whether the needle is in the vein. **2.** Inhale cigarette smoke deeply.

dream *n.* **1.** Opium. See OPIUM. **2.** Morphine. See MORPHINE.

dreamer *n.* Opium or morphine addict.

dried out *adj.* (d) Having withdrawn from a drug, usually in the confines of a hospital.

drive on Expression meaning to continue doing what

one is presently occupied with; don't be distracted. Similar to go head on.

drive over something *v.* (B) Ignore; avoid. **a.k.a.** shine, shine on.

drive up *v.* Induce a state of mental stimulation or agitation via drugs or verbal harassment.

driven up *adj.* Tense; anxious; up tight.

driver *n.* (d) Amphetamine. See AMPHETAMINE.

drop *v.* ingest or swallow any drug. Commonly used in reference to LSD—eg. *I just dropped the reds.* *n.* Narcotics sale in which the drugs are picked up after the money has been paid. See HAND TO HAND.

drop it *v.* **1.** Say it; express what is on your mind—eg. *Drop it on me.* **2.** Stop talking about that.

drop out *v.* **1.** Withdraw from anything that is disliked, such as school, society, responsibilities. **2.** Totally withdraw from the everyday realities of life. Can be via drugs.

dropper *n.* (d) Medicine dropper used as a syringe for injecting drugs. It is easier to manipulate than a hypodermic.

drug dependence *n.* State of psychic and/or physical dependence on a drug arising in a person following the continued use of that drug.

druggie *n.* (d) College student who indiscriminately experiments with drugs for the effects. See DOPE FIEND; DOPER; DOPIE.

drum *n.* A virile Black male. Originated from the name of a fictitious literary character.

drunk *adj.* Under the influence of drugs or alcohol. See LOADED.

drunk tank *n.* (p) Large prison cell where all intoxicated prisoners are kept.

dry fuck *v.* Go through the motions of sexual intercourse without entering the vagina, usually with clothes on. Performed by junior-high-school and high-school students. *n.* The simulated act of sexual intercourse with clothes on.

dry out *v.* (d) Take a cure; discontinue addiction to drugs. See TAKE A CURE.

dubee *n.* **1.** (d) Marijuana cigarette. **a.k.a.** duby. See MARIJUANA CIGARETTE. **2.** (B) Car. See CAR.

duby See DUBEE.

dude *n.* A male.

dujer *n.* (d) Heroin. See HEROIN.

duji (dōō'-gē) *n.* (d) Heroin. See HEROIN.

duke in *v.* (d) Expose an undercover operator, eg., a narcotics agent.

dum dum *n.* Stupid fool; idiot.

dummy *n.* (d) Substance that is supposed to be a narcotic but isn't. It is some other substance, such as milk sugar or talcum powder, designed to fool the buyer. **a.k.a.** blank, turkey. See CUT.

dump *v.* **1.** Have a bowel movement; shit. **2.** Vomit. See VOMIT.

dump on *v.* Be extremely cruel verbally to another person; yell or shout at someone, usually when it is undeserved.

dump the ping in wing *v.* (d) Give up one's plans for an injection.

duros (*Spanish* dōō'-rōs) *n.* High-quality marijuana. See MARIJUANA.

dust *v.* (d) Make a cigarette of a mixture of drugs, usually marijuana and heroin or opium and hashish. See A-BOMB. *n.* Money. See MONEY.

dusted *adj.* (d) Completely fucked-up on hog. See ANGEL DUST; HOG; PCP.

dyke *n.* (h) Lesbian. See LESBIAN.

dynamite *n.* **1.** (d) Marijuana or heroin. **2.** (d) High-quality narcotics. **3.** Exclamation of excitement or pleasure—eg. *That's dynamite!* or *Dynamite!*

e

easy mark *n.* individual who is easily tricked, conned. **a.k.a.** fish, mark, sucker. See CON.

easy rider *n.* Man who marries and/or lives off a prostitute's earnings.

eat *v.* **1.** (d) Take Methedrine. See AMPHETAMINE; METHEDRINE. **2.** Engage in oral-genital sex. See ORAL COPULATION.

eat out *v.* Engage in oral-genital sex. See ORAL COPULATION.

ego death *n.* Total depersonalization; complete dissolution of ego intactness; feeling of being nobody. Often precipitated by a bad drug experience, usually a hallucinogen.

ego games *n.* **1.** The placing of oneself and one's own needs and wants as the most important, with no concern for others. **2.** (d) Depreciative term applied by drug users to social conformity and normal activities and responsibilities of the majority of people, work and organization. Originated with Dr. Timothy Leary.

ego trip *n.* **1.** Activities that are so involved with oneself that one has no concern or consideration for any others. **2.** Activities that are for the purpose of building one's ego, image or reputation—eg. *He's on an ego trip.*

eighth *n.* Eighth of an ounce of a powdered drug. See QUANTITIES OF DRUGS.

electric *adj.* Implying psychedelic cult or drug effects —eg. *electric banana, electric Kool-Aid* (Kool-Aid spiked with LSD). See PSYCHEDELIC.

en ganchos (*Spanish* en gahn'-chōs) *adj.* **1.** Addicted to, hooked on drugs. **2.** High on drugs.

en juanado (*Spanish* en wah-nah'-dō) *adj.* Under the influence of marijuana. **a.k.a.** en leñado, en motado, en yedado.

en leñado (*Spanish* en len-yah′-dō) *adj.* Under the influence of marijuana. **a.k.a.** en juanado, en motado, en yedado. See LEÑO.

en motado (*Spanish* en mō-tah′-dō) *adj.* Under the influence of marijuana. **a.k.a.** en juanado, en leñado, en yedado. See MOTA.

en yedado (*Spanish* en ye-dah′-dō) *adj.* Under the influence of marijuana. **a.k.a.** en juanado, en leñado, en motado. See YEDO.

end up on cold turkey Expression meaning sent away for an abrupt cure; withdrawal from an addictive narcotic. See COLD TURKEY.

ends *n.* Money. See MONEY.

Equanil *n.* (med) (meprobamate; Wyeth Laboratories) Equanil is medically used as a tranquilizer, muscle relaxer, and in rehabilitating alcoholics. Physical or psychic dependence may occur. It is one of the few tranquilizers that is physically addictive with excessive use. Meprobamate is also marketed by another manufacturer under the name of Miltown (Wallace).

esa (*Spanish* e′sāh) *n.* **1.** Dame; tough chick. **2.** Form of address to a female—eg. *See you later, esa.*

ese (e′sā) *n.* **1.** Guy; tough guy. **2.** Form of address to a male—eg. *See you later, ese.* **3.** A Mexican. Term used by whites.

ese bato (*Spanish* e′-sā vah′-tō) *n.* **1.** Literal translation: that guy. A tough guy; a Mexican, Mexican-American. Term used by whites. See BATO. **2.** Hi! or Hello friend! Common in Mexican-American community.

Eskatrol *n.* (d) (dextroamphetamine; Smith, Kline & French Laboratories) Eskatrol is medically used to treat obesity. See AMPHETAMINE.

Establishment *n.* Those who hold positions of power and authority, such as politicians, police, teachers, etc.; the dictators of conventional attitudes and values, and those attitudes and values themselves. The Establishment's way of life is regarded by the underground as undesirable because of the lack of freedom and the hypocrisy. This hypocrisy is the double standard of accepting any activity if it furthers one's own cause and maintains the status quo while condemning similar activities when performed by those not part of the Establishment. An example of this is the excessive use of drugs with the excuse of being for tension, dieting and sleeping while condemning as immoral the use of similar drugs in non-Establishment people. See UNDERGROUND.

ethyl chloride (eth'-əl klo'-rīd) *n.* (d) Anesthesia in spray form sprayed into a cloth and inhaled. A way to get high. The effect lasts less than a minute but use can cause loss of consciousness. A prescription is needed.

Evan *n.* **1.** Someone you love very much; someone whom you wish to spend time with. **2.** A very bright, smart, enjoyable young man.

experience *n.* **1.** (d) Effects of a drug; the things one feels from a drug. **2.** Something that intensely affects a person emotionally. Can be positive or negative. **3.** Something really unusual, out of the ordinary; something that interrupts routine. Can be positive or negative. See TRIP.

explorer's club *n.* (d) Small circle of LSD users who were intellectually experimenting and mind exploring with the drug before it became popular and illegal. Everything was fully planned in advance: time, place, quantity, participants. Most participants were intellectuals and professionals.

f

F. you Fuck you. A very insulting remark. **a.k.a.** F.U. See FUCK; FUCK YOU.

face off *v.* Stand up and face a person one is arguing with as a prelude to a physical altercation.

factory *n.* (d) Equipment used for preparing and injecting drugs. See FIT.

fag *n.* **1.** (h) Male homosexual; effeminate male. See HOMOSEXUAL. **2.** British slang for cigarette. **a.k.a.** faggot.

fag hag *n.* (h) A woman who is attracted to male homosexuals.

faggot *n.* **1.** (h) Male homosexual; effeminate male. See HOMOSEXUAL. **2.** British slang for cigarette. **a.k.a.** fag.

fairy *n.* (h) Male homosexual. See HOMOSEXUAL.

fairy dust *n.* (d) See PCP.

faith, keep the See KEEP THE FAITH (BABY).

fall out *v.* **1.** (d) Go into a form of half sleep while under the influence of a drug, usually a barbiturate or an opiate. See NOD; ON THE NOD. **2.** Go to sleep. Can be but not always caused by use of drugs. **a.k.a.** crash, flake out.

family jewels *n.* Male sex organs. Very old term.

far out *adj.* **1.** Out of the ordinary in a pleasing way; exciting. **2.** Weird; strange; rare; unusual. **a.k.a.** freaky, kinky, way out. **3.** Mentally or emotionally unstable.

fart *v.* Emit gas through the anus. **a.k.a.** let one. *n.* Emission of gas through the anus, often accompanied by a noise. **a.k.a.** peo.

fay *n.* (B) Derogatory term for a white person. **a.k.a.** ofay, peckawood. *adj.* (h) Describes a male homosexual. **a.k.a.** gay, sweet. See HOMOSEXUAL.

fecal freak *n.* One who obtains sexual gratification by ingesting fecal matter, shit. **a.k.a.** brown bov.

fed *n.* Agent of Federal Bureau of Narcotics or any Federal law enforcement agency. See FUZZ; NARC; NARCO; SAM; WISHER.

fellatio *n.* Oral copulation of the penis. **a.k.a.** blowjob, pipe job. See CUNNILINGUS; ORAL COPULATION.

fem *n.* (h) Lesbian who plays the female role in the homosexual match. See LESBIAN.

female *n.* Woman. **a.k.a.** babe, baby, bag, bash, beaver, bird, bitch, broad, bush, chick, crack, cunt, douche, fish, fox, frail, garbage can, heffer, pussy cat, quail, ruca, scag, snatch, stallion, slave, sweet meat, tail, trick, tuna. See GIRL FRIEND; WIFE.

fence *n.* (p) Person who buys stolen goods from the one who steals them and then sells them for a profit.

fiend *n.* (d) Addict (any kind of drugs)—eg. *He's a dope fiend.*

fierro (*Spanish* fē-e′-rō) *n.* **1.** Weapon. **2.** Penny. **a.k.a.** calo, clemo. **3.** Money. See MONEY.

fila (*Spanish* fē′-lah) *n.* Knife.

filoriandro (*Spanish*) *adj.* Presently using or addicted to narcotics, usually heroin.

fine stuff *n.* (d) Narcotics of very good quality.

finger *v.* **1.** Perform masturbation of the vagina. **2.** Identify an individual to the authorities or to anyone; point a person out, eg., discover an undercover agent—*Joe fingered Bill as being a narc.*

finger, the *n.* The middle finger raised with the other fingers bent. Means fuck you. See FUCK YOU!

finger fuck *v.* Stimulate the female sex organs with the finger; insert the finger into the vagina, simulating intercourse. **a.k.a.** bang. *n.* Stimulation of the female sex organs with the finger. See FINGER JOB.

finger job *n.* Use of the finger to caress and insert into the vagina and/or anus (male and female). See FINGER FUCK.

F-ing *v.* Fucking; having sexual intercourse. This term is common to adolescents who still feel uncomfortable using the word "fuck."

F-ing around *v.* Goofing off. This expression is common to adolescents who still feel uncomfortable using the word "fuck."

finger pop *v.* (B) Snap one's fingers to a musical rhythm. Johnny Otis popularized a song called "Finger Poppin' (Time)."

fink *n.* **1.** Squealer; informer. **2.** Creep.

fink out on *v.* **1.** Fail to do something; stand someone up; make a promise and fail to keep it. **a.k.a.** cop out on. **2.** (p) Inform. **a.k.a.** squeal.

fire on *v.* Attack verbally or physically.

fire up *v.* (d) Smoke marijuana.

fish *n.* **1.** Female. See FEMALE. **2.** (p) Inmate. May come from fact that inmates are put into cells that are called tanks. **3.** Easily deceived person. **a.k.a.** easy mark, mark, sucker. See CON. **4.** (h) Male homosexual word for woman.

fish heading for the piddle Expression meaning (1) surrender to the police or (2) gain admittance to a hospital to withdraw from drugs. See CURE, THE; LEXINGTON.

fishwife *n.* (h) Male homosexual's real wife.

fit *n.* Equipment used for preparing and injecting drugs. Consists of a needle, a form of syringe, a bent spoon, a ball of cotton, and sometimes a small bottle of alcohol or perfume for sterilization purposes. **a.k.a.** artillery, business, factory, gear, gimmick, Jim Johnson, kit, layout, machinery, outfit, tools, works. See COOK; SUPPLIES.

five-cent paper *n.* (d) Usually five dollars' worth of a powdered drug that is packaged in a folded piece of paper or a packet. **a.k.a.** five-dollar bag, nickel bag. See QUANTITIES OF DRUGS.

five-dollar bag *n.* (d) Five dollars' worth of a powdered drug in a packet or folded piece of paper. **a.k.a.** five-cent paper, nickel bag. See QUANTITIES OF DRUGS.

fix *v.* (d) Inject—eg. *He just fixed.* *n.* (d) **1.** An injection of a narcotic and the procedures involved —eg. *I need a fix.* See INJECTION. **2.** Amount of drugs that is sold in a bag or packet. See BAG; PACKET; QUANTITIES OF DRUGS.

fixate *v.* (d) Stare fixedly at an object or person while under the influence of a drug.

flake *n.* (d) Cocaine. See COCAINE.

flake out *v.* (d) Pass out; fall asleep. **a.k.a.** crash, fall out.

flaky *adj.* **1.** Mentally unbalanced; crazy; dinghy. **2.** Free; easygoing; hanging loose—eg. *I want a flaky chick.*

flam *v.* Be aggressive; flirt with; come on strong to someone. *n.* Deceitful façade. Comes from flim-flam. **a.k.a.** front, put on, scam. See FLIM FLAM.

flaming *adj.* Word that intensifies any noun—eg. *a flaming groover, a flaming fag.*

flash *v.* **1.** (d) Feel the sudden, initial effects after taking a drug. **2.** (d) Hallucinate—*I just flashed that I was dead.* **3.** (d) Have a sudden thought or insight. **4.** Sniff glue. **5.** Vomit. See VOMIT. *n.* (d) **1.** Sudden, initial feeling after taking a drug. **a.k.a.** jolt, rush. **2.** Hallucination; visual experience. **3.** Sudden thought or insight—eg. *I just had a flash.*

flashback *n.* (d) Recurrence of LSD-induced sensations while not on the drug. These feelings or sensations can be brought to mind by something that was associated with the sensation while on the drug.

flat *n.* **1.** (d) Tablet of LSD. Comes from the appearance of the tablet. **2.** (d) Home; house or apartment. See HOME. *adj.* **1.** Depressed; down. **2.** Flat-chested; small-breasted (female).

flea powder *n.* (d) Poor-quality narcotics.

flick *n.* Movie.

flim-flam *n.* Line, lie, trick used to manipulate someone out of money. There was a movie called *The Flim-Flam Man,* a story of living without working, by using con games. **a.k.a.** con game.

flip *v.* **1.** Have an emotional breakdown. Can be due to drugs. **a.k.a.** flip out, snap. **2.** Have a wild or unusual experience—eg. *Let's go flip.* **3.** Be overcome with excitement or enthusiasm. **a.k.a.** flip out, wig out. **4.** Like or be attracted to someone very much—eg. *I really flipped about (or over) him.*

flip flop *v.* Simultaneous oral copulation of each other by two people. **a.k.a.** 69. See LOOP-DE-LOOP; ORAL COPULATION.

flip out *v.* **1.** Be unable or not want to relate to the social scene because of behavior problems, often directly or indirectly related to a drug experience. **a.k.a.** flip. **2.** Lose one's grasp on reality; have an emotional breakdown. **a.k.a.** flip, snap. **3.** Become very excited about something. **a.k.a.** flip, wig out. **4.** Lose one's temper.

flipped out *adj.* **1.** Not able or willing to relate to the social scene because of behavior problems. **2.** No longer in touch with reality. **3.** Very excited about something. **a.k.a.** wigged out. **4.** Angry.

flit *n.* (h) Homosexual; effeminate male. See HOMOSEXUAL.

float *v.* (d) Be under the influence of drugs. See HIGH.

flower *n.* The philosophy of the flower comes from the fact that a flower is among the most natural of all things in nature; it is free, needing nothing more than earth, air and sunshine to live. It is peaceful and beautiful and gives its beauty freely; it symbolizes peace, friendship, love, sharing and non-competitiveness. It is from this concept that certain people have taken their philosophy and patterned their lives. See FLOWER CHILDREN; FLOWER POWER.

flower children *n.* Those people who attempt to live by the flower philosophy, often using drugs, especially hallucinogens. They reject those existing, socially acceptable methods of obtaining influence or power and prefer a non-commercial, nonmaterialistic approach to life. See FLOWER; FLOWER POWER.

flower people See FLOWER CHILDREN.

flower power *n.* Refers to the ability to affect change through peace, as opposed to the power of coercion, force and violence.

flunky *n.* One who performs minor tasks and runs errands for someone above him in social status or (d) for drug dealers in order to obtain drugs as payment. **a.k.a.** fool.

flush *v.* (d) Flush drugs down the toilet to avoid seizure and arrest by the police. Usually occurs upon hearing a loud knock at the door.

flushed *adj.* Having money. **a.k.a.** heeled.

fly *v.* **1.** (d) Take narcotics. **2.** (d) Feel the effects of a drug. **a.k.a.** fly high. *n.* Aphrodisiac. Comes from Spanish fly.

fly high *v.* (d) Feel the effects of a drug—eg. *He's flying high.* **a.k.a.** fly.

flying saucer *n.* (d) Morning-glory seed. See MORNING-GLORY SEED.

focus *n.* (d) Narcotics solution ready for injection.

foil *n.* (d) Small package of drugs. See BAG.

fool *n.* (d) **1.** One who takes large risks (steals) to acquire money to buy drugs. **2.** One who performs small tasks for a drug dealer in order to obtain drugs. **a.k.a.** flunky.

foolish powder *n.* (d) Powdered drug.

football *n.* (d) Amphetamine; an upper. See AMPHETAMINE.

forward *n.* (d) Amphetamine; an upper. See AMPHETAMINE.

foul *adj.* **1.** Noxious; low-down; deceitful. **2.** Unfair; wrong—eg. *That sure is foul.*

fox *n.* Extremely attractive female—eg. *I got a real fox tonight.* See FEMALE.

foxy *adj.* Desirable; attractive. Refers to a female.

fracture *v.* **1.** Shake up; disturb. **2.** Beat up; clobber.

fractured *adj.* **1.** Angry. **2.** Disturbed; upset. **3.** Extremely amused. **4.** Drunk. See LOADED.

frail *n.* Female. See FEMALE. *adj.* Unintelligent; slow; weak in the head.

frajo (*Spanish* frah'-hō) *n.* Cigarette.

frantic *adj.* (d) In a state of panic, usually because of a desire for narcotics and being unable to procure any.

freak *v.* **1.** (d) Have a very beautiful or very bad drug experience. **2.** (d) Be out of touch with reality due to a bad drug experience. **a.k.a.** freak out. **3.** Shock people by appearance or behavior. *n.* **1.** One whose appearance and behavior are quite noticeable and shocking to the Establishment, the straight people. See ESTABLISHMENT; STRAIGHT. **2.** (d) One who uses drugs. **3.** (d) One who prefers a certain drug and takes it more often than others —eg. *He's an acid freak.* By extending the drug definition, it can mean one who prefers and is involved with a certain philosophy or activity— eg. *She's an anti-war freak.* **4.** One who engages in unusual or deviant sexual activities. **a.k.a.** freak trick.

freak freely *v.* (d) Behave spontaneously and uninhibitedly while under the influence of a drug.

freak off *v.* (d) Engage in any and all sexual activity; engage in unusual or deviant sexual activity. See FREAK; FREAK TRICK.

freak out *v.* **1.** Be out of touch with reality. **2.** (d) Have an emotional breakdown due to a bad drug experience. **a.k.a.** freak. *n.* **1.** Gathering or experience where people do whatever they feel like doing very uninhibitedly, such as taking drugs. **2.** A bad experience.

freak rock *n.* Electric or electronic-sounding music, implying psychedelic. **a.k.a.** acid rock. See HARD ROCK; PSYCHEDELIC.

freak trick *n.* (pr) Man who buys a prostitute and engages in unusual or deviant sexual activities, eg., masturbating while holding an ice cube. **a.k.a.** freak.

freak up *v.* Act in a strange and obvious manner to attract attention.

freaky *adj.* Very strange; unusual. **a.k.a.** far out, kinky, way out. See FREAK.

free clinic *n.* Clinic that is staffed by volunteer personnel who give medical, psychological and employment aid to hippies and to those who cannot afford to pay for these services.

Freep *n.* The *Free Press,* a Los Angeles underground newspaper. Many hippies and dopers sell the *Free Press* on the streets in Los Angeles. See UNDERGROUND.

Freeper *n.* One who habitually reads the *Free Press.* See FREEP.

freeze on me, don't See DON'T FREEZE ON ME.

french *v.* To kiss with the tongue inside the other's mouth. *n.* (pr) Term used by clients of a prostitute to ask for the act of oral copulation.

French blue *n.* (d) Mixture of an amphetamine and a barbiturate, injected. See SPEEDBALL.

French tickler *n.* Prophylactic with soft protruding "petals" on the end. Used to tickle the inner part of the vagina for increased sexual stimulation.

fresh and sweet *adj.* (p) Just out of jail.

fresh merchandise *n.* (d) Anything stolen to furnish funds for purchasing drugs.

frisk *v.* Search. Usually used in reference to police action.

front *v.* (d, pr) Pay in advance for drugs or prostitutes. *n.* **1.** False image one presents to others. **a.k.a.** flam, put on, scam. **2.** Respectable person who represents a group and imparts to it an appearance of success or legality; legal activities used to mask illegal ones. **3.** Head of a group or gang.

front, out See OUT FRONT.

front, up See UP FRONT.

fruit *n.* Homosexual. See HOMOSEXUAL.

F.S.U. *n.* Freak Student Union. See FREAK.

F-13 *n.* Drugs; dope.

F.U. Fuck you. A very insulting remark. **a.k.a.** F. you. See FUCK; FUCK YOU.

fuck *v.* **1.** Have sexual intercourse. See COPULATE. **2.** Ruin; spoil. **3.** Mix up.

fuck around *v.* Fool around; goof off; mess around; fail to be serious.

fuck head *n.* **1.** One who doesn't think very clearly; one who is emotionally confused. **2.** Unreliable person. **a.k.a.** fuck off, shit head. **3.** Person who keeps talking while the author is trying to concentrate.

fuck off *v.* Act foolishly and stupidly. *n.* Unreliable person. **a.k.a.** fuck head, shit head.

fuck over *v.* **1.** Take advantage of someone. **2.** Beat someone up. **3.** Search (by the police).

fuck someone's mind *v.* To persuade forcefully without regard for the feelings of those being persuaded. See MIND FUCKER.

fuck up *v.* **1.** Make a gross error. **a.k.a.** mess up. **2.** (d) Fall completely under the influence of a drug or alcohol. *n.* Unstable person who makes many mistakes.

fuck you Derogatory expression similar in meaning to "go to hell" but much stronger. Usually said in a very hostile manner. **a.k.a.** F. you, F.U.

fucked *adj.* **1.** In bad shape; messed up; confused. **2.** (d) Under the influence of a drug. See LOADED.

fucked over *adj.* Been searched (by the police).

fucked up *adj.* **1.** On the wrong track; stupid; unable to think clearly. **2.** (d) Under the influence of a drug. See LOADED.

fudge *n.* Fudge cooked with marijuana in it. Gives a high, as does smoking marijuana. Marijuana is also cooked in brownies, spaghetti and other things. See ALICE B. TOKLAS.

fumble *v.* (B) Fail to fulfill expected responsibilities; fail to take care of business.

funked out *adj.* (d) Under the influence of a drug. See LOADED.

funky *adj.* **1.** Groovy; with it; in with the times—eg. *She's a funky chick.* **2.** Down to earth. **3.** Describes smells that are repugnant. **4.** Describes raw (deal).

funny farm *n.* Mental hospital or institution.

furburger *n.* Female's pubic area. Comes from fur, referring to the hair, and burger, because one "eats" it (engages in oral-genital activity). See BUSH; EAT; EAT OUT; ORAL COPULATION.

fuzz *n.* **1.** Policeman. See POLICEMAN. **2.** Narcotics agent. **a.k.a.** narc, narco, sam, wisher. See FED.

g

gabacho (*Spanish* gah-vah′-chō) *n.* American; white person. See GRINGO.

gacho (*Spanish* gah′-chō) *adj.* Stingy.

gage *n.* (d) Marijuana. See MARIJUANA.

game *v.* Be dishonest, untruthful, defensive; con; stick to a story when everyone knows it is not valid or passable—eg. *Don't game me. n.* **1.** Interrelationship between people who have accepted certain set responses to their accepted role expectancies—eg. *They're playing a game with each other.* **2.** Synanon game: form of group therapy practiced at Synanon Foundation. See SYNANON FOUNDATION. *adj.* Be ready for, willing to do something—*Are you game?*

gang bang *n.* Act of sexual intercourse by a single female with a number of males at the same time or in immediate succession. See BANG; MAMA; PULL A TRAIN.

gangster *n.* (d) **1.** Marijuana. See MARIJUANA. **2.** User of marijuana. **a.k.a.** pothead.

ganji (gan′-jē) *n.* Type of marijuana or hashish. See HASHISH; MARIJUANA.

gap up *v.* (d) Fill capsules with powdered drugs.

gape *v.* (d) Go through withdrawal symptoms, usually from an opiate. See WITHDRAWAL.

gar *n.* Derogatory word meaning Negro. Shortened form of the word "nigger."

garbage *n.* **1.** Small talk; unmeaningful conversation. **a.k.a.** bull, bullshit, jive. **2.** (d) Low-quality drug. **3.** (d) The residue after cooking some drugs. **4.** (d) Amphetamine; an upper. See AMPHETAMINE. **5.** Everything about oneself; the inner faults—eg. *Put out the garbage.*

gas *v.* Sniff gasoline fumes to get high. *n.* **1.** Good,

exciting, happy event or feeling. **2.** An exclamation—eg. *It's a gas!* **a.k.a.** groove.
gasoline *n.* The fumes are inhaled and the effect is similar to glue sniffing. This can cause brain damage.
gasser *n.* Unusual or astounding occurrence or thought—eg. *That was a gasser.*
gassy *adj.* Good; great; fantastic. See GROOVY.
gauge *n.* (d) Marijuana. See MARIJUANA.
gay *adj.* Homosexual. **a.k.a.** fay, sweet. See HOMOSEXUAL.
gay bar *n.* Bar frequented by homosexuals.
G.B. *n.* (d) **1.** Goofball. **a.k.a.** spansula, speedball. See GOOFBALL. **2.** Amphetamine. See AMPHETAMINE.
gear *n.* (d) Equipment used for preparing and injecting drugs. See FIT.
gee head *n.* Paregoric addict. **a.k.a.** gheid. See HEAD; PAREGORIC.
geed up *adj.* (d) Under the influence of a drug; high. See LOADED.
geeze *v.* (d) Inject a drug—eg. *Have you already geezed?*
geezer *n.* Small quantity of narcotics. See QUANTITIES OF DRUGS.
george *adj.* All right; O.K.
get a glow on *v.* Get high—eg. *He's got a glow on.* See GLOW.
get behind it *v.* **1.** (d) Enjoy a high that is induced by a drug. **2.** Be totally involved in the action at hand—eg. *He can get behind almost any situation.*
get behind the gun *v.* (p) Take a jail sentence if caught.
get down *v.* (B) Fight. **a.k.a.** thump.
get down with it *v.* (B) Start to do something; be serious about doing something.
get high *v.* (d) Take a drug to feel the euphoriant effects.
get in the wind *v.* **1.** (m) Get on one's motorcycle and leave, ride. See LEAVE. **2.** Drive very fast in a car. **a.k.a.** blow it off, blow it out.

get into her pants Expression meaning to have sexual relations with a female. See COPULATE.

get into (it) v. Commence action; get started—eg. *I couldn't study before, but I finally got into it.*

get into someone v. **1.** Become aware of another's thoughts and motivations; be cognizant of another person or thing. **2.** Have sexual relations with (a female). See COPULATE.

get it on v. **1.** Have sexual intercourse. See COPULATE. **2.** (d) Take drugs. **3.** Go, leave. See LEAVE.

get it together v. **1.** Prepare to leave a place. **2.** Clarify thoughts, both emotionally and intellectually.

get off v. **1.** (d) Take a drug. **2.** (d) Begin to experience the first effects of a drug after taking it, also successfully experiencing it—eg. *Did you get off?* **3.** Have a climax (sexual).

get off my case (B) Expression meaning leave me alone. **a.k.a.** Give someone some slack, lighten up.

get on v. (d) Smoke marijuana. See TURN ON.

get one's nuts off v. **1.** Ejaculate; climax (male). From nuts, which are testicles. **a.k.a.** come, cream, cum. **2.** Obtain sexual intercourse; sex for the purpose of climax only, not to please one's partner. **3.** Masturbate to climax. See MASTURBATE.

get some v. Obtain sexual intercourse with someone—eg. *I'd like to get some tonight.*

get some round eye v. Put the penis or the tongue into another's anus. Common activity among prisoners. From round eye, which means anus. **a.k.a.** mix your peanut butter, ram.

get straight v. **1.** (d) Get off drugs. **a.k.a.** go straight. See STRAIGHT. **2.** (d) Get high on drugs. **3.** Go from a homosexual relationship to a heterosexual relationship. **a.k.a.** go straight. See STRAIGHT.

get wasted v. **1.** Get high or drunk. **2.** Take an overdose of narcotics.

ghedis n. Money. See MONEY.

gheid n. (d) Paregoric user. **a.k.a.** gee head. See PAREGORIC.

gibbs n. Mouth—eg. *He hides his drugs in his gibbs.*

gig *n.* Originally a jazz term. **1.** Job. **a.k.a.** slave. **2.** Party. **3.** Interest; hobby.

giggle smoke *n.* (d) Marijuana. See MARIJUANA.

giggle weed *n.* (d) Marijuana. See MARIJUANA.

gimme five Expression said upon giving a specific handshake that originated in the Black community. One person puts a hand out, palm up, and the other person slaps it. Done as a salutation or a sign of approval and/or agreement. **a.k.a.** gimme some skin. See HAND SLAP.

gimme some skin See GIMME FIVE.

gimmick *n.* Equipment used for preparing and injecting drugs. See FIT.

gingus bag *n.* The middle-class dilemma, way of life. See MISTER CHARLIE.

ginseng (*Chinese* ji'-nsen) *n.* Root of ginseng plant, found in Northern China. The oldest medicinal herb of the Orient, it is used as a curative for a variety of illnesses to restore a sense of alertness, and well-being. Word literally means man-root. **a.k.a.** natural speed.

girl *n.* (d) Cocaine. Term used mostly in the U.S. See COCAINE.

girl friend *n.* **a.k.a.** best piece, better half, hope to die, main squeeze, old lady, piece, woman.

give head *v.* Engage in oral copulation. See ORAL COPULATION.

give me librium, or give me meth (d) A parody of Patrick Henry's famous statement. Librium is a tranquilizer; meth is Methedrine.

give someone some slack *v.* Refrain from pressuring or confronting another. **a.k.a.** get off my case, lighten up.

glad rag *n.* Handkerchief saturated with a drug in order to sniff it.

glasshouse *n.* (p) Los Angeles term for jail. Comes from Los Angeles County Jail's glass-dominated construction.

gleep *v.* Insult.

globe *n.* Female's breast. See BREAST.

glow *n.* (d) Euphoric feeling derived from taking a drug. **a.k.a.** high. See GET A GLOW ON.

glue *n.* (d) Common model-airplane glue inhaled to obtain a high feeling. This procedure is extremely dangerous, more so than the use of most drugs; it causes organic brain damage. See GLUE SNIFF.

glue sniff *v.* (d) Inhale model-airplane glue. Resultant effects are double vision, slurred speech, poor coordination, feeling of euphoria, and hallucinations. Glue sniffing is regarded as an adolescent type of drug abuse, but it causes organic brain damage, and it can cause liver, kidney and bone-marrow damage. Eventually most glue sniffers outgrow glue and go to more adult-type drugs such as marijuana, LSD, barbiturates, amphetamines or heroin. Since late 1969 most glue manufacturers have been experimenting with combining the glue with a mustard-smelling compound that would make the odor too repugnant to sniff while not hindering normal use of the glue.

go down on *v.* Engage in oral-genital sex. See ORAL COPULATION.

go head on Expression meaning (1) continue with what you are doing; (2) go head; start; take action; (3) agreement with someone's action or plan, often passive. See HEAD ON.

go on with your bad self (B) Expression said to someone who is doing something he does not ordinarily do or exaggerating something he normally does. A positive, encouraging statement.

go out? wanna See WANNA GO OUT?

go straight *v.* **1.** (d) Get off drugs. **a.k.a.** get straight. See STRAIGHT. **2.** Change from homosexual to heterosexual relationships. **a.k.a.** get straight. See STRAIGHT. **3.** Abstain from illegal activities; live within the law. See STRAIGHT.

go through changes *v.* Change one's attitudes or actions after the realization of something; be anxious or tense because of something. See CHANGES; PUT SOMEONE THROUGH CHANGES.

go to it Expression meaning (1) be really involved; engrossed in what one is doing—eg. *I was really going to it and he interrupted me.* **a.k.a.** go at it; (2) stop procrastinating and commence action; (3) become involved in an action at hand; (4) go on; do your thing; enjoy yourself.

go up *v.* **1.** (d) Begin to be under the influence of a drug; become high. **2.** (mu) Make a mistake in playing the music.

going down *v.* Happening—eg. *What's been going down?*

going down, what's been See WHAT'S BEEN GOING DOWN.

gold *n.* (d) Very high quality marijuana. Short for Acapulco gold or Panama gold. See MARIJUANA.

gold dust *n.* (d) Cocaine. See COCAINE.

golden leaf *n.* (d) Marijuana. Comes from Acapulco gold. See MARIJUANA.

golden shower boy *n.* One who obtains sexual gratification by ingesting urine.

gong *n.* (d) Opium pipe.

gong beater *n.* Opium smoker.

gong, kick the See KICK THE GONG.

good go *n.* (d) Fair quantity of a drug received for the payment.

good people *n.* **1.** O.K. person—eg. *He's really good people.* **2.** (d) One who can be trusted with drugs.

good stuff *n.* (d) High-quality drugs. From stuff, which means drugs.

goods *n.* (d) Any form of drug.

goody *n.* A person who does *everything* properly and according to the rules (to an obnoxious extent). May come from goody-goody. **a.k.a.** goody-goody, goody two-shoes.

goody-goody *n.* A person who does *everything* properly and according to the rules (to an obnoxious extent). **a.k.a.** goody, goody two-shoes. *adj.* Extremely good; behaving according to the rules; always doing everything right; pure (to an obnoxious extent)—eg. *He's too goody-goody for me.*

goody two-shoes *n.* A person who appears to be or is playing the role of always being overly good, sincere, understanding, forgiving, pure (to an obnoxious extent). **a.k.a.** goody, goody-goody.

goof *v.* **1.** Make a mistake. **a.k.a.** goof up, mess up. **2.** (d) Take drugs. **3.** Do something just for the sake of doing it. **a.k.a.** goof around, goof off, mess around. **4.** Play practical jokes on someone. *n.* Mistake; error.

goof around *v.* Do something just for the sake of doing it. **a.k.a.** goof, goof around, mess around.

goof off *v.* Do something just for the sake of doing it. **a.k.a.** goof, goof around, mess around.

goof on someone *v.* Become absorbed in watching another person.

goof up *v.* Make a mistake. **a.k.a.** goof, mess up.

goofball *n.* **1.** Mixture of cocaine and heroin. **a.k.a.** G.B., speedball. **2.** Mixture of barbiturates and amphetamines. **a.k.a.** G.B., spansula, speedball. **3.** Amphetamine, usually Benzedrine. See AMPHETAMINE; BENZEDRINE. **4.** Person who "goofs off." Obsolete usage.

goofed up *adj.* **1.** Unable to function; confused; disoriented. **2.** (d) Under the influence of a narcotic. See LOADED.

goofer *n.* (d) One who takes pills.

grass *n.* (d) Marijuana. See MARIJUANA.

grasshopper *n.* (d) User of marijuana.

gravy *n.* (d) Mixture of blood and heroin that is reheated because it has coagulated in the syringe and can't be injected.

grease *v.* Eat. **a.k.a.** peck.

grease and soul *n.* (B) **1.** Soul music. **2.** Soul food. **3.** Sweat. See SOUL.

greaser *n.* Derogatory term for Mexican, Mexican-American.

green *n.* Money. See MONEY. *adj.* Never tried something—*eg. When it comes to playing guitar, he's green.*

green dragon *n.* Amphetamine; an upper. See AMPHETAMINE.

grefa n. (d) Marijuana. From the Spanish *grifa*. See MARIJUANA.

greta *n.* (d) Marijuana. See MARIJUANA.

grey *n.* (d) White person.

greybar hotel *n.* (p) Jail.

greyboy *n.* (d) White male.

grifa (*Spanish* grē'-fah) *n.* Marijuana. See MARIJUANA.

griffa *n.* (d) Marijuana. See MARIJUANA.

griffo *n.* (d) Marijuana. See MARIJUANA.

grind *n.* Leg.

gringo (*Spanish* grēn'-gō) *n.* American; white person. Can be derogatory. **a.k.a.** gabacho, paddy, pale face, patty, whitey.

grip *v.* (B) Masturbate. See MASTURBATE.

groove *v.* Tune in; feel harmony with; be on the same wavelength with. *n.* **1.** Good thing or experience. The connotation is that of joy and happiness. **2.** Exclamation—eg. *What a groove!* **a.k.a.** gas.

groove, in the See IN THE GROOVE.

groove on *v.* Like very much—eg. *I groove on what's going on* or *I really groove on him.*

groover *n.* **1.** Person who likes acid-rock music and psychedelic things. See ACID ROCK; PSYCHEDELIC. **2.** (d) Person who gets high on drugs.

groovy *adj.* **1.** Great; fantastic; joyful; happy. **a.k.a.** bitchen, bon-a-roo, boss, gassy, out of sight, right on, smokey, spiffie, spiffy, super, tits, wicked, wiggy. **2.** (d) Describes the euphoric feeling from a drug—eg. *I'm feeling groovy.* **3.** Expression meaning O.K., I agree.

gross *adj.* Disgusting; unspeakable—eg. *That was a gross thing to do.*

group grope *n.* Group of people engaged in sexual play, but not intercourse; petting. See PET.

groupie *n.* Girl (teenybopper) who makes herself sexually available to the guys in musical bands. Some girls even live with the guys whenever they are in town. They hang around the discotheques; the managers of the discotheques like having them around because they are usually attractive, dress very wildly (freaky) and dance well. A potential hazard involved is, of course, venereal disease.

groupnik *n.* Individual who is totally engrossed in the processes of group interaction. Many have no other social contacts, but merely attend different groups every night, ie., group therapy, encounter groups, T groups, sensitivity groups.

guide *n.* Person who attends or sits with an LSD user during an experience. **a.k.a.** guru, sitter, tour guide.

gum *n.* A substance on which to get high. Soft mint-flavored gum is wrapped around banana peel; the whole is enclosed in green pepper, wrapped in aluminum foil, and put in a dark place for six weeks. It is then baked at 200° F. for two hours and the crust is scrapped and smoked. From *The Hippy's Handbook,* by Ruth Bronsteen.

gum it *v.* **1.** Oral copulation of the vagina. See CUNNILINGUS; ORAL COPULATION. **2.** Oral copulation done without teeth. See ORAL COPULATION.

gun *n.* Eyedropper or syringe that is considered part of the equipment for the preparation and injection of a drug. May also refer to the needle. See FIT.

gun, get behind the See GET BEHIND THE GUN.

gunji (gun'jah, gun'jē) *n.* (d) Opium. See OPIUM.

gunny *n.* (d) Marijuana. See MARIJUANA.

guru (gōō'-roo, gə-ru') *n.* **1.** Wise man; one who teaches or guides. A term from India, associated with spiritual awareness. **2.** (d) Person who sits with an LSD user during an experience. **a.k.a.** guide, sitter, tour guide.

guru-you Parody on the expression "screw you," which means fuck you. Common use in universities. See FUCK YOU.

guzzled *adj.* (p) Arrested.

h

H *n.* (d) Heroin. See HEROIN.

H and C *n.* (d) Heroin and cocaine. **a.k.a.** hot and cold.

habit *n.* (d) Addiction to drugs; inability to function without a drug, usually heroin. Described in terms of the cost of the physically necessary daily quantity—eg. *He's got a $25.00-a-day habit.*

hack *v.* Cope with; tolerate; stand—eg. *I can't hack my job.* *n.* (p) Prison guard.

hacked *adj.* Angry. **a.k.a.** hacked off, pissed, pissed at, pissed off (at).

hacked off *adj.* Angry. **a.k.a.** hacked, pissed, pissed at, pissed off (at).

had, been See BEEN HAD.

Haight See HAIGHT-ASHBURY.

Haight-Ashbury Area in San Francisco known for its population of drug-oriented anti-Establishment individuals, or hippies. Communal living is common in the area. Because of the unusual dress and appearance in general of the people who live there, the area is frequented by tourists. See COMMUNE; ESTABLISHMENT.

hair *n.* **1.** Latest style originated among young anti-Establishment men is very long hair (shoulder length or longer) and a return to beards, mustaches and sideburns. Long hair is considered a part of one's masculinity among the users of heroin and other hard drugs partly because the sexual expression of masculinity is minimal, since sex is a very small part of their lives due to decreased sexual desire caused by the drugs. Long hair is an expression of rejection of the fact that in our society one is judged in a superficial way in regard to masculinity, femininity and status. Long hair visibly identifies one's predisposition toward the subculture's values. Many professional, relatively Establishment-oriented people are now wearing their hair longer than a few years ago and wearing sideburns, beards and mustaches. There is a visual experience caused by long hair being shaken while tossing the head that is associated with drug taking and the performances of acid-rock musical groups. See ACID-ROCK; ESTABLISHMENT; HARD DRUG; HIPPY. **2.** Strength; courage **a.k.a.** balls, cojones, juice.

HAIR! "American Tribal Love Rock" musical popular in many countries where local professional companies are presenting it in the language of the country. Its tone is that of the anti-Establishment way of life. It employs new forms of theater, such as nudity and audience participation. Even though the lyrics are anti-Establishment, the songs have been accepted and are played in all levels of society.

hairburger *n.* **1.** Vagina. **a.k.a.** HAIRPIE. See VAGINA. **2.** Female's pubic area. Hair refers to the pubic hair and burger comes from the idea of eating it, which means oral copulation. See BUSH; EAT; EAT OUT; ORAL COPULATION.

hairpie *n.* **1.** Vagina. **a.k.a.** HAIRBURGER. See VAGINA. **2.** Female's pubic area. Hair refers to the pubic hair and pie comes from the idea of eating it, which means oral copulation. See BUSH; EAT; EAT OUT; ORAL COPULATION.

hairy *adj.* **1.** Difficult to deal with; heavy. See HEAVY. **2.** Unusual; frightening—eg. *It was a hairy book.*

half and half *n.* (pr) Term used by clients of a prostitute to obtain half of her time with oral copulation and half with sexual intercourse.

half can *n.* Amount of narcotic equivalent to half a Prince Albert tobacco can. **a.k.a.** 1/2 can, matchbox. See QUANTITIES OF DRUGS.

half piece *n.* (d) One-half ounce of heroin. See QUANTITIES OF DRUGS.

hallucinogen (hə-lōō′-ci-nə-jen) *n.* (med) Drug tnat

produces visual hallucinations similar to those experienced by psychotic patients. The difference is that the drug user usually realizes that his hallucinations are caused by the drug and are not real. The hallucinogenic drugs are not physically addictive, but the pleasant and unusual experiences from the drugs tend to create a psychological need for continued use. Recurrent hallucinations may occur in some people for a period of time after use of the drugs; these are called flashbacks or flashes. If the drug user has persistent and continuous flashes, and no longer knows they are drug-induced, he may go into a psychotic state. This may also occur during the drug experience if the user loses the realization that the hallucinations are from the drug and considers them to be real. Some hallucinogenic drugs are LSD and its derivatives, mescaline, peyote and psilocybin. See ARATHWA; DIETHYLTRYPTAMINE; DIMETHYLTRYPTAMINE; DIPROPYLPHYPTAMINE; DOM; HAWAIIAN PODS; LYSERGIC ACID DIETHYLAMIDE; MAGIC MUSHROOM; MARIJUANA; MESCALINE; PEYOTE; PSILOCYBIN; SACRED MUSHROOM; STP.

ham *n.* (B) Black male. **a.k.a.** home boy.

hand slap *n.* (B) Type of handshake that originated in the Black community. One person puts a hand out, palm up, and the other person slaps it. Done as a greeting and also as a sign of approval and/or agreement. Often accompanied by the expression "Gimme five" or "Gimme some skin." See GIMME FIVE.

hand to hand *adj.* (d) Describes person-to-person delivery of narcotics at the time the money is paid. See DROP.

handle (something) *v.* **1.** Be able to cope with a situation—eg. *Can you handle it?* or *I can't handle working there anymore.* **2.** Be aware of what is happening in a particular situation. **3.** Be in the for—eg. *Can you handle a steak now?*

hang

hang *v.* Disappoint another; stand someone up. **a.k.a.** cuff, hang up.

hang in (there) Expression meaning to continue, keep strong in a stressful situation. **a.k.a.** hang tough.

hang it up Expression meaning (1) forget it; (2) let's give up; (3) stop.

hang loose Expression meaning (1) relax; remain calm; (2) wait—eg. *Hang loose till he gets here;* (3) take things as they come; don't always plan.

hang tough Expression meaning don't give up. It is used to encourage individuals during a stressful situation, such as a period of withdrawal from a drug. Hang tough was commonly used at Synanon Foundation during the foundation's initial stages when addicts were allowed to withdraw after entering Synanon. Synanon's house in Santa Monica, California, has a ship's white life preserver upon which is written "S.S. *Hang Tough*" hanging on the wall. **a.k.a.** hang in (there). See SYNANON FOUNDATION; WITHDRAWAL.

hang up *v.* Disappoint another person; stand a person up; withdraw from a commitment—eg. *He really hung me up.* **a.k.a.** cuff, hang. *n.* Problem with no apparent immediate answer, usually repetitive in nature. See HUNG UP.

hap *n.* Occurrence of interest that is going on. From the word "happening"—eg. *Where is the hap?* **a.k.a.** scam.

happening *n.* Event; a spontaneous event. The word also refers to a planned gathering where spontaneous activities occur; people do whatever they feel like doing, sometimes only for themselves and sometimes to entertain others.

happening? what's See WHAT'S HAPPENING?

happy dust *n.* (d) Cocaine. Dust refers to the powdered condition of the drug. See COCAINE.

hard drug *n.* (d) A physically addictive drug, eg. heroin, morphine, opium and their derivatives. **a.k.a.** hard stuff, heavy drug, heavy stuff. See LIGHT STUFF; SOFT DRUG.

hard rock *n.* Rock-'n'-roll music with a very prominent beat and repeated sounds. See ACID ROCK; FREAK ROCK.

hard stuff *n.* (d) A physically addictive drug. Stuff means drug. **a.k.a.** hard drug, heavy drug, heavy stuff. See LIGHT STUFF; SOFT DRUG.

harness bull *n.* Uniformed police officer.

harp *n.* **1.** Musical instrument. **2.** Harmonica.

harry *n.* (d) Heroin. See HEROIN.

hash *n.* Hashish. See HASHISH.

Hashbury *n.* (d) Haight-Ashbury district of San Francisco, called Hashbury as a play on words between hashish and Ashbury Street. See HASHISH.

hashish (ha'-shēsh) *n.* The resin, the most potent part, of the female marijuana plant, which is compressed and then smoked. It is more expensive than common marijuana. The darkness determines its strength. It is not physically addictive. One ounce of hashish is about equivalent to one pound of marijuana. **a.k.a.** black Russian, chunks, ganji, hash, South African hash.

hassle *v.* **1.** (d) Buy drugs with some difficulty. See PANIC. **2.** Argue or disagree with someone—eg. *We hassled about money.* *n.* Annoyance; conflict situation.

hat it up *v.* (B) Leave; depart. See LEAVE.

have designs on a person *v.* Be interested in; be attracted to. Usually has a sexual connotation.

have moths in one's pocket Implies holes in one's pocket, so everything falls through. Therefore is applied to a person who is irresponsible, unable to follow through with commitments—eg. *He has moths in his pocket.* Originated from cartoon where character opens pocketbook and moths fly out.

have the stumbles *v.* (d) Stumble due to the effect of a drug; lose balance; be awkward; be uncoordinated.

have you hit him? Question meaning have you asked him for whatever you wanted.

Hawaiian pods

Hawaiian pods *n.* A hallucinogen stronger than LSD. See HALLUCINOGEN.

hawk *n.* **1.** (d) User of LSD **2.** (d) Seller of LSD **3.** (B) In Chicago, among Blacks, this term refers to the very fast cutting wind during the winter, which makes life very unpleasant for the poor with run-down living quarters and no heat. Lou Rawls popularized the word in one of his songs.

hay *n.* (d) Marijuana. See MARIJUANA.

hayhead *n.* (d) User of marijuana. See HEAD.

head *n.* **1.** (d) Word used with a drug to denote one who frequently uses and prefers that drug—eg. *pothead, acid head.* **2.** Narcotic user, usually marijuana or LSD. **3.** Oral copulation: give head. See ORAL COPULATION. **4.** Rest room. **5.** Leader.

head drug *n.* (d) Drug that stimulates the brain and alters one's state of consciousness and is not physically addictive, such as a hallucinogen. It is to be differentiated from a body drug, which is a physically addictive drug. See HALLUCINOGEN.

head job *n.* Oral copulation. See ORAL COPULATION.

head on *v.* Go; go ahead; do it. Comes from go head on. See GO HEAD ON.

head shop *n.* Store, usually small, where unusual items and drug utensils can be bought. Caters to the psychedelic, with such things as strobe lights, water pipes, posters, roach clips, etc. See HEAD.

head shrinker *n.* Psychologist; psychiatrist. **a.k.a.** psych, shrink.

head thing *n.* Emotional involvement, more than a sexual relationship, with an individual, usually of the opposite sex—eg. *He had a head thing where she was concerned.* See SOUL ROLL.

heart *n.* (d) **1.** Dexamyl. See AMPHETAMINE; BARBITURATE; DEXAMYL. **2.** Dexedrine. See AMPHETAMINE; DEXEDRINE. **a.k.a.** cartwheel, rose. See AMPHETAMINE.

heat *n.* **1.** Police. See POLICE. **2.** Pressure—eg. *The heat's on.* **3.** Firearm; gun. From criminals' old word for gun—heater. See PIECE.

heave *v.* Vomit. See VOMIT.

heavenly blue *n.* Morning-glory seed. See MORNING-GLORY SEED.

heavy *n.* Bad guy; a mean person—eg. *He made me look like the heavy.* *adj.* **1.** Very good; meaningful; deep—eg. *He uses heavy words* or *They have a very heavy relationship.* **2.** Bad; disturbing—eg. *He gave us a heavy ultimatum.* See HAIRY. **3.** Pregnant.

heavy drug *n.* (d) An addictive drug. **a.k.a.** hard drug, hard stuff, heavy stuff. See LIGHT STUFF; SOFT DRUG.

heavy stuff *n.* (d) An addictive drug. Stuff means drug. **a.k.a.** hard drug, hard stuff, heavy drug. See LIGHT STUFF; SOFT DRUG.

heavyweight Jones *n.* (d) One who sells drugs with aim of getting someone strung out.

heeled *adj.* **1.** Having money—eg. *He's well heeled.* **a.k.a.** flushed. **2.** (d) Having drugs. **a.k.a.** dirty, holding.

heifer *n.* (B) Young cow; derogatory term for female. See FEMALE.

heist *n.* (p) Robbery.

hemp *n.* Marijuana. See MARIJUANA.

henry *n.* (d) Heroin. See HEROIN.

hep *adj.* Aware; informed; knowledgeable; in with the times; with a comprehension of. Hep is less commonly used than is hip. **a.k.a.** hip, in.

hepatitis, serum See SERUM HEPATITIS.

her *n.* (d) Cocaine. See COCAINE.

herbie *n.* Establishment-type person, very conventional in attitude. **a.k.a.** Mister Charlie, Mister Jones. See ESTABLISHMENT.

hero (*Spanish* e'-rō) *n.* Heroin. Common term in Mexican-American community. See HEROIN.

heroin *n.* (med) (diacetylmorphine hydrochloride) A semisynthetic derivative of morphine but five times stronger. It has a duration of action of four hours. Heroin is a strong depressant. It is a white or light-brown odorless crystalline powder with

heroin

a bitter taste. Heroin comes from the opium poppy (*Papaver somniferum*) which is grown legally in the hills of Turkey. The opium is processed into crude morphine and then is smuggled into France and converted into heroin in illegal but sophisticated laboratories. From France it is smuggled into the U.S., usually by the Mafia, which controls about 80% of the drug market in the U.S. Heroin is taken by injection directly into a vein or by sniffing. Sniffing does not satisfy the need of the addict and he usually goes on to inject it subcutaneously and eventually intravenously. The body develops a tolerance to heroin and the addict must increase the amount he uses. Since he is unable to determine the strength of what he buys, he must increase the number of times he injects the drug to maintain the constantly increasing dosage used. Drowsiness, constipation, nausea and urinary retention are common effects as are contraction of pupils, slow pulse and respiration, loss of appetite and sexual drive. Overdose may cause coma and death from respiratory failure. Heroin is highly physically addictive and as soon as the effects of one injection wear off, the body begins to crave the drug. If no drug is introduced, the addict begins to experience withdrawal. Withdrawal from heroin is extremely painful, therefore the addict's entire life is usually spent in pursuit of the drug. Since it is expensive and so often needed, most male addicts commonly steal or rob and most female addicts commonly become prostitutes. Methadone is sometimes substituted for heroin, but methadone is as addicting as heroin. **a.k.a.** big H, boy, brown stuff, china white, chiva, dogie, dojee, dojie, doojee, doojer, dooji, dujer, duji, dynamite, 8, H, harry, henry, hero, him, horse, junk, lemonade, poison, salt, scag, scat, schmack, schmeck, shit, shmeck, shmee, smack, snow, stuff, tecata, white, the white lady, white stuff. See WITHDRAWAL.

he-she *n.* Homosexual. See HOMOSEXUAL.
hi-ball *n.* Benzedrine; Dexedrine. See AMPHETAMINE; BENZEDRINE; DEXEDRINE.
hickey *n.* Mark made on the skin by biting and sucking during sexual play. Often seen on the neck. **a.k.a.** monkey bite.
high *n.* An exhilarating feeling; happy state. Not necessarily induced by drugs. **a.k.a.** glow. *adj.* (d) **1.** Stimulated or depressed by drugs or alcohol; under the influence of drugs or alcohol. See LOADED. **2.** Very happy.
high (ways to get) See alcohol (surgical spirit), banana peel, catnip, chew five-day deodorant pads, ethyl chloride, glue, gum, lettuce, millet seed, morning-glory seeds, mucara, nutmeg, periwinkle leaves, tea. From: *The Hippy's Handbook,* by Ruth Bronsteen. Also: Sniffing of breath freshener, cleaning fluids, gasoline, glue, lacquer, nail-polish remover, oven cleaner, paint, shoe polish.
high place, be in a See BE IN A HIGH PLACE.
high yellow *n.* (B) Light-skinned Black person; a mixture of races.
hike *v.* Make a quick transaction.
him *n.* (d) Heroin. See HEROIN.
hip *adj.* Aware; knowledgeable; informed; wise; with a comprehension of; in tune with the times. **a.k.a.** hep, in.
hippie See HIPPY.
hippy *n.* **1.** Predominantly middle-class white youth, ranging in age from about 12 to 25. It seems they are exclusively heterosexual. Some drop out of society, do not work, take drugs, have long hair, dress non-conventionally and live communally. Many are interested in the aspects of Eastern mystic philosophies that stress quietness, withdrawal, meditation and they avoid aggression and competitiveness. Some consider drugs a short cut to the enlightenment of Eastern religions. **a.k.a.** hippie. See COMMUNE; DROP OUT; FLOWER CHILDREN. **2.** Person who is in tune with the modern psyche-

hit *v.* **1.** (d) Inject a drug into a vein. **a.k.a.** line, mainline. **2.** (d) Obtain drugs. **3.** Steal; rob. *n.* **1.** Dose of a drug. **a.k.a.** strike. **2.** An injection of a narcotic. See INJECTION. **3.** (d) Puff of a marijuana cigarette. **4.** Sexual intercourse. See COPULATION.

hit on someone *v.* **1.** Ask for a favor. **2.** Steal from. **3.** Flirt with. **4.** Get something from someone. **5.** Trick. **a.k.a.** con. See CON GAME.

hit the moon *v.* Reach the highest part of a drug experience. Comes from the idea of feeling as though one is flying and is at the height, which is the moon. **a.k.a.** peak. See REACH FOR THE MOON; THERE.

hitch *v.* Hitchhike. **a.k.a.** thumb.

hock *v.* Obtain a loan on an object of value at a pawnshop. **a.k.a.** pawn.

hog *n.* **1.** (d) Addict who uses more than he needs to get high. **2.** Addict who requires large doses of drugs. **3.** Big car, especially the '55 or '56 Buick. See CAR. **4.** (m) Motorcycle. **5.** (d) Phenanthrene, a synthetic drug having much the same effect as PCP. It is addictive. See ANGEL DUST; PCP.

hold *v.* **1.** (d) Carry drugs; have drugs in your possession—eg. *He's holding.* **a.k.a.** carry. **2.** (d) Have drugs for sale. **3.** Masturbate. See MASTURBATE.

hold your mud *v.* (p) **1.** Not inform to the police when questioned. **2.** Not give out any information to anyone.

holding *adj.* (d) Possessing narcotics. **a.k.a.** dirty, heeled.

hole *n.* **1.** Tobacco cigarette. **a.k.a.** dirt, square, square joint, straight. **2.** (p) Solitary confinement in prison. See IN THE HOLE.

hole, in the See IN THE HOLE.

home *n.* **a.k.a.** crib, crow's nest, flat, pad, stompin' ground.

home boy *n.* (B) Black male. **a.k.a.** ham.

homosexual *n.* Person who engages in sexual activities and love relationships with members of the same sex. Most commonly used to refer to a male; lesbian refers to a female homosexual. Some homosexuals have marriage-type relationships; one partner takes on the characteristics and plays the role of the male and one the female. An example of this can be seen in the motion picture *Staircase*. **a.k.a.** con, fag, faggot, fairy, flit, fruit, he-she, joto, lesbian, maricón, nellie fag, punk, queen, queer, sissy. See AC-DC; BI; CLOSET CASE; CLOSET QUEEN; LESBIAN; TRANSVESTITE. *Adj.* Displaying sexual interest in a person of the same sex. **a.k.a.** fay, gay, sweet.

honalee (hahn'-ə-lē) *v.* (d) Get high on heroin. From the song "Puff (The Magic Dragon)"; Puff lived in "Honalee"—eg. *Did you honalee?*

honcho *n.* Powerful person, both physically and mentally.

honeymoon *n.* (d) Period when normal doses of a drug are taken.

honkie See HONKY.

honky *n.* (B) Derogatory term for a white person. Originated in Harlem. **a.k.a.** honkie.

hookah (hook'-ə) *n.* (d) Pipe for marijuana, hashish or opium smoking. It is Eastern in origin. The pipe has a part that is filled with water to cool the smoke. **a.k.a.** pipe, poopkie, steamboat, toke pipe, water pipe.

hooked *adj.* Addicted to a drug physically and/or psychologically, usually to an opiate.

hooker *n.* Prostitute. See PROSTITUTE.

hoopdee *n.* (B) Latest-model car.

hop head *n.* (d) User of narcotics, usually heroin or morphine. See HEAD.

hope city *n.* (d) State of euphoria obtained through drugs.

hope to die *n.* (B) Spouse; girl friend or boy friend. See GIRL FRIEND; WIFE.

horn

horn *v.* Inhale through the nostrils. **a.k.a.** blow the bag, sniff, snort.

horny *adj.* Need of a sexual release, especially through relations with another person.

horrors *n.* (d) Terrifying dreams and hallucinations caused by taking drugs, particularly an amphetamine or cocaine—eg. *He's got the horrors.*

horse *n.* (d) Heroin. **a.k.a.** caballo. See HEROIN.

horse and buggy *n.* (d) Needle and medicine dropper used for injecting drugs. See FIT.

hot *adj.* **1.** Sexually aroused. **2.** Stolen—eg. *This watch is hot.*

hot and cold *n.* (d) Heroin and cocaine. Comes from the fact that heroin and cocaine are opposites; heroin depresses the body and cocaine tends to stimulate it. **a.k.a.** H and C.

hot rod *v.* (B) Masturbate. See MASTURBATE.

hot shot *n.* (d) **1.** Injection of poison that user believes to be good drugs, a method of getting rid of police informers. **2.** Injection of a drug that is of higher potency than the addict is accustomed to, usually causing him to respond as if it were an overdose.

hot turkey *v.* (d) Ignite an entire marijuana cigarette or the end portion of it and sniff the fumes given off.

hotel *n.* **1.** (p) Jail. See CLINK. **2.** (pr) Dwelling of a prostitute.

house *n.* **1.** (p) Jail. See CLINK. **2.** (pr) Place where prostitutes are available.

how did you make out? Expression meaning (1) how did you do? or (2) what was the outcome?

huelga (*Spanish* wel'-gah) *n.* Strike (in the sense of workers' stopping work as a protest against low wages and poor working conditions).

huevos (*Spanish* wā'-vōs) *n.* Testicles. See TESTICLES.

hum job *n.* Oral copulation. Can be by putting another's testicles in one's mouth and humming, causing a pleasurable sensation. See HUMMER; ORAL COPULATION.

hummer *n.* **1.** (p) An arrest on suspicion—eg. *They pinned a hummer on me.* See BUSTED BUT NOT TWISTED. **2.** A phony; a fake. **3.** One who engages in oral copulation. See ORAL COPULATION. **4.** One who engages in oral copulation of the testicles by putting them in the mouth and humming to cause vibrations that are pleasurable. See HUM JOB; ORAL COPULATION.

hump *v.* Have sexual intercourse. See COPULATE.

hung up *adj.* **1.** Unable to reach a decision. **2.** Hopelessly involved with something or someone—eg. *I am hung up on that chick.* **3.** Very neurotic; confused; having many problems. See HANG UP.

hung up on *adj.* Very attached to; involved with a person or thing. Can be positive or negative—eg. *I'm really hung up on Fred.*

hungry *adj.* In need of money.

hungry croaker *n.* (d) Doctor who sells drug prescriptions to addicts. From hungry, which means in need of money. **a.k.a.** croaker.

hurting *adj.* Lacking something, eg., looks, intelligence, money.

hustle *v.* **1.** Attempt to obtain money, sex or drugs through illicit, quasi-legal activities, con games. See CON; CON GAME; HUSTLER. **2.** Sell drugs. **3.** Take advantage of. See CON. **4.** (pr) Sell oneself as a prostitute.

hustler *n.* **1.** One who attempts to obtain money using tricks and lies. In the drug subculture, a good hustler is admired a great deal because of his ability to continue his operations successfully without getting caught. See CON; CON GAME; HUSTLE. **2.** (pr) Prostitute. See PROSTITUTE.

hype *v.* Create a sham situation; swindle. See CON. *n.* **1.** (d) Person who injects drugs. Comes from hypodermic. **2.** Lie; untrue story. **3.** A swindle. **a.k.a.** con game.

hypnotic *n.* (med) Drug that produces sleep. *adj.* Producing sleep.

i

I can dig it Expression meaning (1) agree with someone or something; (2) like something; (3) understand.

ice cream *n.* (d) Opium. See OPIUM.

ice cream habit *n.* (d) Occasional use of drugs.

ice cream man *n.* (d) Opium seller.

ice in one's shoes (d) Expression meaning that one is refraining from using a drug because of fear.

ice pack *n.* High-quality marijuana. See MARIJUANA.

ice tong *n.* Medical doctor.

ice tray *v.* (d) Smoke hashish or marijuana over an ice tray covered with tin foil. The ice is used in order to make the smoke cooler.

iceberg *n.* (d) Marijuana that has been smuggled into Los Angeles with iceberg lettuce. Term common to Los Angeles only. See MARIJUANA.

Illinois green *n.* Marijuana. **a.k.a.** Chicago green. See MARIJUANA.

I.M. *adj.* (med) Intramuscular. Describes an injection given in the muscle as opposed to in the vein.

I'm way down Expression meaning I need some drugs. Commonly refers to marijuana.

I'm whipping (B) Expression meaning really doing something well, working hard; working out.

in *adj.* **1.** Socially acceptable within a subculture. **2.** In tune with the modern scene **a.k.a.** hep, hip.

in drag *adj.* (h) In the clothing of the opposite sex, trying to appear to be a member of the opposite sex.

in power adj. (d) Having drugs to sell, usually heroin.

in stir In jail.

in the groove In tune with, knowledgeable about what's going on.

in the hole 1. (p) In solitary confinement in prison. **a.k.a.** on the shelf. **2.** In trouble.

in transit *adj.* Under the influence of LSD.

incense *n.* Substance burned to produce fragrance in the air. The odor is quite strong and is used to overcome the odor given off by burning hashish or marijuana or just for a pleasurable scent. Much incense comes from India and became popular in the U.S. with the rising interest in Eastern mystic religions. It is very popular among young people, even non-drug-users.

Indian hay n. (d) Marijuana. See MARIJUANA.

Indian hemp *n.* The generic term for marijuana. See MARIJUANA.

inhalers n. (d) Substances such as airplane glue that are inhaled for their deliriant effects.

injection *n.* Forcing of a fluid into the body **a.k.a.** bang, boot, fix, hit, jolt, make, pop, shot, tom, tom mix.

instant Zen *n.* (d) LSD. Called instant Zen because it gives the same type of insights and revelations that are associated with Zen. See HALLUCINOGEN; LYSERGIC ACID DIETHYLAMIDE; ZEN.

International Society for Krishna Consciousness *n.* Mystic religious group, India-oriented, whose main religious exercise is chanting "Hare Krishna . . ." In Hollywood, California, groups of followers dressed in pale-orange "togas," the men with partially shaven heads, stand along the sidewalk, usually in the evening, playing tambourines, chanting and attempting to get converts.

into (something) *adj.* Involved; interested; preoccupied —eg. *I'm really into poetry now.*

intramuscular (in'-trah-mus'-kyə-lər) *adj.* (med) Directly into the muscle. Used to describe an injection. **a.k.a.** I.M.

intravenous (in-trah-vēn'-əs) *adj.* (med) Directly into the vein. Used to describe an injection. **a.k.a.** I.V. See MAINLINE.

Irvine *n.* Policeman; cop. See POLICEMAN.

I.U.D. *n.* (med) Intrauterine device, a birth control device, usually coillike in appearance, that is inserted by a physician into the uterus **a.k.a.** coil. See CONTRACEPTIVE.

I.V. *adj.* (med) Intravenous. Describes an injection given in the vein as opposed to in the muscle. See MAINLINE.

j

J *n.* (d) Marijuana cigarette. See MARIJUANA CIGARETTE.

J smoke *n.* (d) Marijuana cigarette. See MARIJUANA CIGARETTE.

jack *v.* (d) Prolong initial effect of a drug by alternately injecting a small amount and then letting the drug and blood back up into the syringe. **a.k.a.** boot, jerk off.

jack off *v.* **1.** Masturbate. See MASTURBATE. **2.** Fool around aimlessly. *n.* Inept or stupid person.

jacked up *adj.* **1.** (d) Under the influence of a drug. Refers to a stimulant or amphetamine. **2.** Overly excited and nervous. **a.k.a.** wired.

jacket (p) File or case history of an individual.

jag *n.* (d) Prolonged state of drug intoxication.

jag off *v.* **1.** Masturbate. See MASTURBATE. **2.** *n.* Inept or stupid person.

jail plant *n.* (d, p) Narcotics concealed on a person for use in jail. See PLANT.

jam *v.* **1.** Depart; leave. See LEAVE. **2.** Have a group gathering. **3.** Lose one's cool; be at a loss for words. **4.** (mu) Play a musical instrument in a group, unrehearsed. *n.* Predicament.

jam session *n.* (mu) Spontaneous gathering of musicians to play, unrehearsed.

jammed up *adj.* (d) Having taken an overdose of a drug.

Japanese beads. See BEADS.

jar *n.* (d) Bottle of 1,000 pills.

jasper *n.* (h) Lesbian. See LESBIAN.

jaws are tight, my See MY JAWS ARE TIGHT.

jay *n.* (d) Marijuana cigarette. See MARIJUANA CIGARETTE.

jay bird *n.* **1.** (p) Person who has been in jail. **a.k.a.** J-bird. **2.** Jewish person. **a.k.a.** J-bird.

jay smoke *n.* (d) Marijuana cigarette. See MARIJUANA CIGARETTE.

jazz *n.* Talk—eg. *I don't want to hear all that jazz.*

jazzed *adj.* **1.** Excited; enthused—eg. *I'm really jazzed about my new car.* **2.** (d) Under the influence of a drug; high. See LOADED.

J-bird 1. Person who has been in jail. **a.k.a.** jay bird **2.** Jewish person. **a.k.a.** jay bird.

jef *v.* Make a mistake.

jeff *v.* (B) Act like an Uncle Tom, a Black man who plays up to a white man. See UNCLE TOM.

jefferson airplane *v.* (d) Sniff or snort a burning marijuana cigarette. *n.* (d) Match that is split and used to hold the end of a marijuana cigarette. The rock group Jefferson Airplane took its name from the above. **a.k.a.** clip, crutch, roach clip.

jelly baby *n.* (d) Amphetamine; an upper. See AMPHETAMINE.

jerk *v.* (B) Have sexual intercourse—eg. *I've been jerking his wife.* See COPULATE.

jerk off *v.* **1.** Masturbate. See MASTURBATE. **2.** (d) Inject a drug a little at a time, letting blood from the vein flow back into the syringe and reinjecting it. This is done to prolong the initial feelings (the rush) and to make sure the needle is in a vein. **a.k.a.** boot, jack.

Jersey green *n.* Type of marijuana. See MARIJUANA.

Jim Johnson *n.* (d) Equipment used for preparing; and injecting drugs. See FIT.

jimson weed *n.* (d) Stramonium. Used in asthma cigarettes. Some people use it to get high.

jissom (ji'-zəm) *n.* (B) Of Biblical origin. **1.** Sperm. **2.** Semen. **a.k.a.** come, cum, load.

jive *v.* Fit in; go with—eg. *It just doesn't jive.* *n.* **1.** (d) Marijuana. See MARIJUANA. **2.** Small talk. **a.k.a.** bull, bullshit, garbage. *adj.* Not acting right; doing something wrong—eg. *You never showed up. You're a jive dude.*

jive stick *n.* (d) Marijuana cigarette. See MARIJUANA CIGARETTE.

job *n.* (d) Injection of a drug. See INJECTION.

jobber *n.* Difficult undertaking—eg. *That's a real jobber.*

job off *n.* (d) **1.** Subcutaneous injection of a narcotic. **a.k.a.** pop, skin, skin pop. **2.** Effect of such an injection.

john *n.* **1.** Bathroom. **a.k.a.** can. **2.** (pr) Man who pays a prostitute for purpose of sexual activity. **a.k.a.** trick.

johnson *n.* (B) Penis. See PENIS.

Johnson grass *n.* (B) Marijuana. See MARIJUANA.

joint *n.* **1.** (d) Home-rolled marijuana cigarette. See MARIJUANA CIGARETTE. **2.** (p) Jail or prison. **3.** Penis. See PENIS. **4.** Run-down place like a restaurant or pool hall.

jolly bean *n.* (d) Amphetamine; an upper. See AMPHETAMINE.

jolt *n.* (d) **1.** An injection of a narcotic. See INJECTION. **2.** Immediate effect derived from an injection of a drug. **a.k.a.** flash, rush, zing.

jones *n.* (d) The habit of a drug addict—eg. *His jones is heavy.*

joto (*Spanish* hō'-tō) *n.* Homosexual; queer. See HOMOSEXUAL.

joy juice *n.* (d) Chloral hydrate. **a.k.a.** Mickey Finn, peter. See CHLORAL HYDRATE.

joy pop *v.* (d) Inject narcotics only occasionally. Comes from pop, which means inject. See CHIP.

joy popper *n.* (d) One who only occasionally injects drugs. A joy popper usually injects the drug subcutaneously (skin pop). See CHIPPY; JOY RIDER.

joy powder *n.* (d) Morphine. See MORPHINE.

joy ride *v.* Steal a car just for a while only to ride in and have fun. Often done by minors too young to have a license.

joy rider *n.* (d) Non-addict who occasionally, but not habitually, takes a drug. **a.k.a.** chippy. See JOY POPPER.

joy smoke *n.* Marijuana. See MARIJUANA.

joy stick *n.* (d) Marijuana cigarette. See MARIJUANA CIGARETTE.

juanita *n.* (d) Marijuana. See MARIJUANA.

jug *n.* **1.** (d) Bottle containing a liquid drug, such as Methedrine. **2.** Female's breast. See BREAST.

juice *n.* **1.** Liquor. **2.** Strength; guts; stamina. **a.k.a.** balls, cojones, hair.

juice head *n.* One who drinks liquor. See HEAD.

juiced *adj.* Intoxicated (from alcohol). See LOADED.

jump on *v.* Castigate someone for some action taken; get on someone's back.

junk *n.* (d) **1.** Heroin. This name has been used since the beginning of the 1900s. See HEROIN; JUNKER; JUNKIE. **2.** Any drug.

junk tank *n.* (p) Prison cell where drug users are kept. Comes from junk, which means drug, and tank, which means cell.

junker *n.* (d) Seller of drugs, usually heroin. Comes from junk, which means heroin. See PUSHER.

junkie *n.* Person who is addicted to heroin. Comes from junk, which means heroin.

juvie *n.* **1.** Juvenile officer. **2.** Juvenile hall.

k

Kama Sutra *n.* Love and sex manual of old India.

kee *n.* (d) 2.2 pounds of marijuana. Word comes from kilogram. **a.k.a.** key, ki. See QUANTITIES OF DRUGS.

Keep off the grass Slogan meaning stay away from or do not use marijuana. When used satirically, it means take marijuana.

keep the faith (baby) Expression said upon departure. Popularized by Adam Clayton Powell during the refusal to seat him in Congress.

keg *v.* Focus on a person; pay attention to someone. *n.* Large barrel of beer.

keif See KIEF.

keister *n.* Rear end.

keister plant *n.* (d) Narcotics hidden in the rectum. See PLANT.

key *n.* (d) 2.2 pounds of marijuana, a quantity by which marijuana is sold. Comes from kilogram. **a.k.a.** kee, ki. See QUANTITIES OF DRUGS.

ki *n.* (d) 2.2 pounds of marijuana. **a.k.a.** kee, key. Comes from kilogram. See QUANTITIES OF DRUGS.

kick *v.* **1.** (d) Stop using drugs. **2.** Complain; object; protest. *n.* Pleasurable emotion; thrill. See KICKS.

kick party *n.* (d) Party where LSD is used.

kick stick *n.* (d) Marijuana cigarette. See MARIJUANA CIGARETTE.

kick the gong *v.* Smoke opium.

kick the habit *v.* (d) Withdraw from an addictive drug, connotes permanently.

kickback *n.* (d) Resumption of drug taking after an extended period of non-use.

kicks *n.* **1.** Fun; good times; good feelings. **2.** Excitement; thrills—eg. *He gets his kicks by riding a motorcycle.* **3.** (d) Pleasurable sensation derived from the use of drugs.

kief (kēf) *n.* (d) Compressed pollen of the marijuana plant; unadulterated hash, without resins. **a.k.a.** keif, kif. See MARIJUANA.

kif See KIEF.

kilo *n.* 2.2 pounds, a quantity by which marijuana is sold. Comes from kilogram.

kinky *adj.* Very strange; unusual **a.k.a.** far out, freaky, way out.

kiss ass *n.* One who attempts to gain approval and acceptance by being exceptionally nice. **a.k.a.** A.K., ass kisser. See BROWN NOSE; KISS SOMEONE'S ASS; KISSY.

kiss someone's ass Expression meaning to attempt to gain approval or acceptance by being exceptionally nice. **a.k.a.** brown nose. See ASS KISSER; KISS ASS; KISSY.

kiss the fish *v.* Smoke hashish.

kissy *adj.* Fawning; kissing up to someone. See ASS KISSER; BROWN NOSE; KISS SOMEONE'S ASS.

kit *n.* (d) Equipment used for preparing and injecting drugs. See FIT.

kite *n.* (d) One ounce of a drug (East Coast usage). See QUANTITIES OF DRUGS.

knock it off Command meaning stop it.

knock on the door *v.* (d) Plan to take a cure, to stop being addicted to drugs. See CURE, THE.

knock up *v.* Get a female pregnant—eg. *He knocked her up* or *She got knocked up*.

knock yourself out Expression meaning (1) have a good time; do your own thing with enthusiasm or (2) work hard.

knocked in *adj.* (d) Arrested for use or possession of marijuana.

knocked out *adj.* **1.** (d) Under the influence of a narcotic. See LOADED. **2.** Unable to function. **3.** Impressed positively about something.

knocked up *adj.* Pregnant—eg. *She's knocked up.*

knocker *n.* Female's breast. See BREAST.

kokomo *n.* Cocaine addict.

K.Y. *n.* (d) Federal hospital in Lexington, Kentucky, that treats drug addicts. Comes from the abbreviation of Kentucky. See CURE, THE; LEXINGTON.

K.Y. jelly *n.* Vaginal lubricant. Term used by prostitutes. Name comes from a brand name.

kype *v.* To steal. **a.k.a.** lift.

L

L *n.* (d) LSD. See HALLUCINOGEN; LYSERGIC ACID DIETHYLAMIDE.

lace *n.* (B) Money. See MONEY.

lace it on *v.* (B) Give money to. **a.k.a.** tie it on.

lacquer *n.* Substance sniffed to obtain a high.

laid back *adj.* Apathetic; uncaring; unconcerned; disinterested—eg. *She is a laid-back chick.*

lame *adj.* **1.** Unaware of the modern situation; lacking knowledge of drugs; naïve in regard to psychedelic activities. **a.k.a.** square. **2.** Establishment-oriented. **a.k.a.** square, straight. See ESTABLISHMENT; MISTER CHARLIE. **3.** Dumb.

later Salutation meaning good-by, see you later.

launching pad *n.* (d) Place to take drugs, get high. **a.k.a.** acid pad, shooting gallery. See PAD.

lay *v.* Have sexual intercourse with. Common to both homosexual and heterosexual relations—eg. *I got laid last night* or *He'd like to lay her.* See COPULATE.

lay down *v.* **1.** Tell or show an attitude or opinion—eg. *I can't go along with what he's laying down.* **2.** (d) Smoke opium in a prone position, the customary position for smoking opium. *n.* Place where opium is smoked.

lay it on *v.* Give something for free, eg., information or an object—eg. *I'll lay it on you.*

lay up *v.* **1.** Stay home for an extended period of time, taking it easy, not doing much. **2.** (d) Stay home for the primary purpose of using drugs; have enough drugs to last for a time so you don't have to go out and buy them.

layout *n.* (d) Equipment used for preparing and injecting drugs. See FIT.

LD-50 *n.* Synthetic cannabinol, active ingredient of marijuana.

leaf, the *n.* (d) Cocaine. See COCAINE.
leaper *n.* Amphetamine. See AMPHETAMINE.
leave *v.* Depart. **a.k.a.** blow, cut, cut out, get in the wind, get it on, hat it up, jam, make the scene, make it, make tracks, pack up, split, slide, splurge, take off, walk.
leg *n.* (B) Sexual intercourse—eg. *Give me some leg.* See COPULATION.
legal high *n.* (d) A high obtained from those substances that are legally obtained and that will affect the user in ways that are similar to prohibited drugs. Some examples are green pepper, banana peel, catnip. **a.k.a.** natural trip.
lemonade *n.* (d) Poor-quality heroin.
leño (*Spanish* len-yō) *n.* High-quality marijuana. See MARIJUANA.
lesbian *n.* (h) Female homosexual. **a.k.a.** dyke, jasper. See BULL DYKE; BUTCH; FEM; HOMOSEXUAL.
let it slide Expression meaning ignore an occurrence, don't take negative action on something.
let one *v.* Emit gas through the anus. **a.k.a.** fart.
let something slide *v.* **1.** Let it go; fail to take care of something; wait. **2.** Let something go by; fail to pay attention to; let someone get away with something.
lettuce *n.* **1.** The milky juice of lettuce can be extracted by blenderizing and is drunk to produce a mild high. **2.** Money (obsolete). See MONEY.
Lex *n.* the United States Public Health Service (Narcotics) Hospital at Lexington, Kentucky. **a.k.a.** Lexington.
Lexington *n.* (d) The United States Public Health Service (Narcotics) Hospital at Lexington, Kentucky. A Federally operated medical center for the treatment and cure of drug addicts. **a.k.a.** Lex. See CURE, THE.
L.F. Lousy fuck. See FUCK.
Librium *n.* (med) (chlordiazepoxide hydrochloride; Roche Laboratories) Fairly mild tranquilizer used primarily to treat anxiety.

lid *n.* **1.** (d) One ounce of marijuana, a quantity by which it is sold. **a.k.a.** can. See QUANTITIES OF DRUGS. **2.** (B) Hat. **a.k.a.** sky piece.

lid popper *n.* (d) Amphetamine. Comes from lid, which means head, and flip one's lid. See AMPHETAMINE.

life the plant *v.* (d) Remove narcotics from their hiding place. See PLANT.

lifer *n.* **1.** (d) Person who takes drugs for most of his life, usually 15 to 20 years. **a.k.a.** carpet walker. **2.** (p) Person who has been sentenced to life in prison.

lift *v.* To steal. **a.k.a.** kype.

lift pill *n.* (d) Amphetamine; an upper. See AMPHETAMINE.

lift up *n.* (d) Feeling while under the influence of drugs—eg. *I'm really on a lift up.*

light *adj.* **1.** Undependable; untrustworthy. **2.** Not too smart.

light show *n.* Effect derived by the simultaneous use of various colored lights shown through and upon various mediums. Light shows are given in auditoriums, coffeehouses, etc. They are put on for the purpose of simulating a hallucinogenic experience. They are usually accompanied by psychedelic music (acid rock).

light stuff *n.* (d) Non-addictive, non-opiate drug such as marijuana. **a.k.a.** soft drug. See HARD DRUG.

light up *v.* **1.** Light a marijuana cigarette. **2.** "Let's smoke [marijuana]."

lighten up *v.* Command meaning get off my back, go easy on me. **a.k.a.** get off my case, give someone some slack.

like 1. Expression used for emphasis or to gain attention to what one is saying—eg. *Like do you understand?* **2.** Expression used in sentences as a filler or hesitation word instead of "uhmm," has no real meaning.

lilly *n.* Seconal. A barbiturate named for the company that makes it. See BARBITURATE; SECONAI

line *v.* (d) Inject a drug directly into a vein. Comes from mainline. **a.k.a.** hit, mainline. *n.* (d) Vein. **a.k.a.** mainline.

link Negro *n.* Black person who is able to function successfully in both the Black and white communities.

lit up *adj.* (d) Under the influence of a narcotic. See LOADED.

lizard *n.* Penis. See PENIS.

load *n.* **1.** (d) Drugs—eg. *He has a load.* **2.** Semen—eg. *I really shot my load.* **a.k.a.** come, cum, jissom.

loaded *adj.* under the influence of drugs or alcohol. **a.k.a.** bent, bent out of shape, blasted, blocked, boxed, drunk, fractured, fucked, fucked up, funked out, geed up, goofed up, high, jazzed, juiced, knocked out, lit up, on, messed up, monolithic, out of it, out of one's mind, ripped, smashed, spaced out, spiked, stiffed, stoned, tight, tore up, torn up, turned on, twisted, wasted, wiped out, wired.

loco *n.* Marijuana. See MARIJUANA. From the Spanish word for crazy.

loner *n.* One who desires to be alone frequently and is accustomed to doing most things alone.

long *adj.* Having an abundance of something, usually narcotics—eg. *He's long on heroin.*

long cut *n.* (d) Intense craving for food, usually sweets. This commonly occurs about a week after a person has stopped using an addictive drug. **a.k.a.** the chucks.

long green *n.* Money. See MONEY.

looking *v.* (d) Wishing to buy drugs.

loop-de-loop *n.* (B) Simultaneous oral-genital copulation between two people. See FLIP FLOP; ORAL COPULATION; 69.

loose *adj.* Sexually promiscuous—eg. *She's really a loose chick.*

Lophophora williamsii (lō-fa-fhō'-ra wil'yəm-zē) *n.* (med) Peyote, a small cactus plant. The tops, or buttons, of the plant resemble mushrooms

lose one's wig

and produce hallucinations when ingested. The main alkaloid in peyote is mescaline. See BUTTON; HALLUCINOGEN; MESCALINE; PEYOTE; TOP.

lose one's wig Expression meaning to lose one's mind. See WIG.

lose your cookies *v.* Vomit. See VOMIT.

lose your cool *v.* Lose control of yourself; get upset; lose your temper. See COOL.

love children See FLOWER; FLOWER CHILDREN.

love handle *n.* The side and back part of the body at waist level where a bulge of fat may be. This bulge can be cupped in the hand and held on to like a handle. (Lateral abdominal wall above the iliac crest; flank fat.)

love in *n.* Gathering of people with the main purpose of loving or taking drugs or singing songs and eating, or all the above, with a share-and-share-alike attitude. See BE IN.

love nuts *n.* Pain in the testicles due to extreme sexual excitement without release through ejaculation. **a.k.a.** blue balls.

love weed *n.* (d) Marijuana. See MARIJUANA.

low *n.* (d) Bad reaction to any drug. *adj.* Depressed; down.

low life *n.* Bum; no good, mean, nasty person—eg. *He's a low life.* **a.k.a.** shit head.

low rider *n.* **1.** Motorcycle rider who has his handle bars raised 16 inches above the legal limit so he looks as though he is riding low. **2.** Person who drives a lowered car. **3.** Bastard.

LSD *n.* (d) Most common name for lysergic acid diethylamide. See HALLUCINOGEN; LYSERGIC ACID DIETHYLAMIDE.

lush *n.* **1.** Very heavy drinker (alcohol). **2.** An alcoholic.

lysergic acid diethylamide (lī-sər'-jik as'-id di-eth'-əl-am-īd') *n.* In full, d-lysergic acid diethylamide tartrate 25; shortened to LSD-25; commonly called LSD. It is a hallucinogenic drug that produces weird, bizarre and unpredictable behavior.

lysergic acid diethylamide

It was first developed by Dr. Albert Hofmann at the Sandoz Laboratories in Switzerland. It is 5,000 times more potent than mescaline and 200 times more potent than psilocybin. The effects vary and are related to the emotional state and the circumstances under which it is taken. (See SET; SETTING.) The effects start about a half hour after ingestion. The first reactions are usually anxiety, dilation of the pupils and a loss of appetite. The hallucinations and other effects last from five to 16 hours. Often they recur (see FLASH; FLASHBACK; RECURRENCE) even while not on the drug. People are rarely very aggressive when on LSD. Serious side effects of this drug are prolonged psychotic effects, paranoia, possible brain damage, possible damage to chromosomes, psychosis and/or suicide. Distortion and intensification of sensory perceptions, especially visual hallucinations, suggestibility and ego-fragmentation are also common. Some of the immediate effects may be offset by administration of strong doses of Thorazine, which reverses LSD's effect and calms the person. LSD is nontoxic and is not physically addictive, but psychic dependence may occur. It is odorless, tasteless and colorless in its pure form. If the drug has an odor, taste or color, it can be attributed to the diluent, mixing agent or impurities in manufacture. It is sometimes mixed with speed. A very small amount will "turn on" a large number of people. This fact inspired the book *The Town That Took a Trip,* by Deane Romano (published by Avon, 1968, #S369). The author writes of an entire town that was turned on by LSD as a prank. A drop of LSD may be taken on a tablet, a sugar cube, gum, cookies (often animal crackers) or in a liquid. It may also be injected. Most people take LSD with another person (see GUIDE), who guides them through their trip, or with a number of other people. Most people who take

lysergic acid diethylamide

LSD are from the college-educated middle class. The reason for taking LSD is often said to be to "expand one's consciousness" and to obtain insights into oneself, and frequently just to have the experience itself. **a.k.a.** A, acid, ácido, the big chief, big D, blue cheer, bluejeans, the chief, cresta, cresto, dome, instant Zen, L, LSD, owsley, pink, pink swirl, purple, purple flat, sugar, sugar lump, 25, ticket, tric acid, trips, twenty-five, wedge, white lightning, Zen. See HALLUCINOGEN.

m

M *n.* (d) **1.** Marijuana. See MARIJUANA. **2.** Morphine. See MORPHINE.

MacArthur Park *n.* Park in downtown Los Angeles. In the song "MacArthur Park," the connotation in the lyrics is that the park is drug-oriented, that drugs can be purchased there. The discussion of "making it" and "baking it" refers to obtaining and taking drugs.

machine *n.* (d) Syringe used for injecting a drug.

machinery *n.* (d) Equipment for preparing and injecting drugs. See FIT.

mack *v.* (pr) Procure clients for a prostitute. Procurer takes a percentage of the prostitute's income. **a.k.a.** pimp.

macro- *adj.* Prefix meaning large—eg. macrobopper= an older teenybopper. See BOPPER.

made it *v.* Achieved one's emotional goal; be where one wants to be. See THERE.

magic mushroom *n.* (d) Mushroom that produces effects similar to LSD when eaten. **a.k.a.** sacred mushroom. See HALLUCINOGEN; PSILOCYBIN; SOMA; TEONANACATL.

main squeeze *n.* **1.** Wife. See WIFE. **2.** Girl friend, on a very intimate level. See GIRL FRIEND.

mainline (d) *v.* Inject drugs directly into a vein. **a.k.a.** hit, line. *n.* Vein of the body, usually in the arm. **a.k.a.** line.

mainliner *n.* (d) Person who injects drugs directly into the vein.

maintain *v.* **1.** (d) Be able to continue to function while using drugs. **2.** Keep control; hold your temper.

make *v.* **1.** Detect something or someone—eg. *I made him as a narcotics agent.* **2.** (d) Buy drugs—eg. *I made him for some pot.* **a.k.a.** cop, make a buy, make a meet, make the man. **3.** Try to have sexual intercourse with—eg. *He tried to make her.* **a.k.a.** put the make on, put the moves on. *n.* **1.** An injection of a narcotic. See INJECTION. **2.** Police check on a person—eg. *They ran a make on him.*

make a buy *v.* (d) Purchase drugs. See MAKE.

make a meet *v.* (d) Purchase drugs. See MAKE.

make a motion *v.* Take a planned action; make a decision—eg. *He made a motion to stop using drugs.*

make a run *v.* (d) Drive to another place (usually Mexico) in order to obtain a large quantity of a drug.

make a strike *v.* (d) Obtain drugs; make a connection. **a.k.a.** score. See CONNECTION.

make it *v.* **1.** Get along well; function within society. **2.** (d) Be on drugs; be using drugs. **3.** Have sexual intercourse. See COPULATE. **4.** Leave. See LEAVE.

make love *v.* Have sexual intercourse. See COPULATE.

make out *v.* Kiss and caress from the neck up. **a.k.a.** neck.

make out? how did you See HOW DID YOU MAKE OUT?

make the man *v.* (d) Buy drugs. See MAKE.

make the scene *v.* **1.** Go where something is happening. **2.** Do something. **3.** leave; depart. See LEAVE. **4.** Have sexual intercourse. See COPULATE.

make tracks *v.* **1.** (d) Leave needle marks on the body from injecting drugs. **2.** (m) Get out; leave; get away. See LEAVE.

mama *n.* (m) One of the girls who are part of a motorcycle gang. She is free to have sexual relations with any member of the gang. She has been initiated into the gang and is trusted. Most females are not trusted by the male members. To become a mama, a girl must have sexual intercourse with each male member (see GANG BANG; PULL A TRAIN). As an "in" member of the gang, the mama's responsibility is to the male members and not to the females who are just fellow travelers and not "in" members.

mama's mellow *n.* Effect of Seconal. See BARBITURATE; SECONAL.

man, the *n.* **1.** Policeman—eg. *The man's here.* See POLICEMAN. **2.** Exclamation of excitement or bewilderment—eg. *Man, that's great!* **3.** (B) White person; boss. **4.** Form of address to a male. **5.** (d) Drug seller or connection.

manicure *v.* (d) Prepare marijuana for use by eliminating all twigs and seeds from it. This is done by placing it in a box cover, tilting slightly and raking through the marijuana until all the seeds and twigs fall to the bottom of the box cover or by straining the marijuana through a screen or flour sifter.

mano (*Spanish* mah'-nō) *n.* Brother. Form of address to close friends. Comes from *hermano,* which means brother. **a.k.a.** carnal.

mantra *n.* A personal word that one repeats over and over again while meditating; form of meditation originally from India.

margarita *n.* (d) Marijuana. See MARIJUANA.

maricón (*Spanish* mah-rē-kɔn') *n.* Homosexual. See HOMOSEXUAL.

marijuana (ma-ri-wah'-na) *n.* Marijuana is the flowering top, stems and leaves of the female Indian hemp plant, whose botanical name is *Cannabis Sativa,* the active element of which is tetrahydrocannabinol. These parts are dried, cleaned of seeds and twigs, and smoked or eaten and can be cooked into brownies, spaghetti or other foods. There is a wide range of quality of the plant. Marijuana is classified as a hallucinogen. Its duration of action is one to six hours. It attacks the central nervous system. Short-term effects create a euphoric high feeling; increased sensory awareness; time/space distortions; increased appetite (especially for sweets); lessening of inhibitions; mild, transient loss of recent memory; and sometimes transient close-connected symptoms of paranoia. It often eliminates feelings of stress and anxiety

marijuana

and lessens depth of concern for emotional problems. It is commonly used as an escape from reality and responsibilities. With the use of marijuana, one's ability to function is slightly impaired and the degree of impairment is directly proportional to the quantity and quality consumed. Marijuana is not physically addictive, but a psychological habit or dependence can develop after chronic use. The physical symptoms are a feeling of heaviness, a buzz in the head, dizziness, dryness of the mouth, reddened eyes, unsteadiness of the body's coordination and a tendency to talk excessively or giggle without provocation. Some people experience nausea and/or vomiting. Most sensations are exaggerated and many people find the pleasure of eating and sexual relations greatly intensified. Heavy use may lead to bronchitis or conjunctivitis; cases of a cannabis psychosis have been reported. It is possible to precipitate schizophrenic reactions in latent schizophrenics. In cases of extreme anxiety or paranoid ideas, chlorpromazine may be administered. **a.k.a.** Acapulco gold, baby bhang, bhang ganjah, black gungi, boo, bush, Canadian black, charas, charge, Chicago black, Chicago green, Congo metaby, dagga, dirt grass, duros, dynamite, gage, gangster, ganji, gauge, giggle smoke, giggle weed, gold, golden leaf, grass, grefa, greta, grifa, griffa, griffo, gunny, hay, hemp, ice pack, iceberg, Illinois green, Indian hay, Indian hemp, Jersey green, jive, Johnson grass, joy smoke, juanita, leño, loco, love weed, M, margarita, marjorie, mary ann, mary jane, mary warner, mary weaver, Mexican brown, Mexican green, Mexican red, michoacan, the mighty mezz, M.J., moocah, mota, mutha, Panama, Panama gold, Panama red, pod, pot, P.R., rainy day woman, rama, red, red dirt marijuana, rough stuff, shit, stum, sweet lucy, T, tea, Texas tea, 13, tosca, yedo, yesca. See CANNIBIS SATIVA; HALLUCINOGEN.

M. D. A.

marijuana cigarette *n.* (d) Cigarette made with marijuana instead of tobacco, **a.k.a.** ace, bomber, cocktail, dubee, duby, J, J smoke, jay, jay smoke, jive stick, joint, joy stick, kick stick, the mighty mezz, muggle, number, pin, reefer, roach, root, spliff, stick, thumb, twist.

marjorie *n.* (d) *Marijuana.* See MARIJUANA.

mark *n.* **1.** Individual who is easily tricked, lied to or conned—eg. *Jack has always been a mark.* **a.k.a.** easy mark, fish, sucker. See CON. **2.** (d) Scar caused by hypodermic injections. See TRACK.

marshmallow *n.* Female's breast. See BREAST.

marshmallows *n.* Testicles. See TESTICLES.

mary *n.* **1.** (h) Form of address by one homosexual to another when the second is effeminate. **2.** (d) Morphine. See MORPHINE.

mary ann *n.* (d) **1.** Marijuana. See MARIJUANA. **2.** Morphine. See MORPHINE.

mary jane *n.* (d) Marijuana. See MARIJUANA.

mary warner *n.* (d) Marijuana. See MARIJUANA.

mary weaver *n.* (d) Marijuana. See MARIJUANA.

masturbate *v.* Stimulate manually the penis or vagina. **a.k.a.** beat off, beat the meat, grip, hold, hot rod, jack off, jag off, jerk off, stroke the lizard.

matchbox *n.* (d) Amount equivalent to half a Prince Albert tobacco can. **a.k.a.** ½ can, half can. See QUANTITIES OF DRUGS.

maxi- *adj.* Prefix meaning larger, older—eg. *maxi-bopper* = an older woman who wears miniskirts. See BOPPER.

mayata (*Spanish* mah-yah′-tah) See MAYATE.

mayate (*Spanish* mah-yah′-tā) *n.* Black person.

Mazola party *n.* Two or more people who get together to engage in sexual play and intercourse with their bodies covered with vegetable oil. This produces a unique sexual sensation. Comes from the brand name of the oil. **a.k.a.** Wesson party.

M.D.A. *n.* (d) Methyl di-amphetamine. See METHYI DI-AMPHETAMINE.

mean *adj.* Very good; perfect; doing something well—eg. *He's a mean ballplayer.*

measurements of drugs. See QUANTITIES OF DRUGS.

medical hype *n.* (d) **1.** One who obtains drugs legally but nevertheless is addicted. Hype refers to one who is addicted to drugs and injects them. **2.** Person whose addiction may have been accidental, started via a doctor's treatment during an illness. Often a result of the doctor's carelessness.

meat *n.* Penis. See PENIS.

meet *n.* An appointment usually used in reference to buying drugs. See MAKE A MEET.

mellow *adj.* **1.** Just good; pleasant; not very high or very low. **2.** (d) Describes feeling one has just as one begins to feel the effects of a drug. **3.** Describes feeling one has just after sexual climax.

mellow dude *n.* Devout drug user.

mellow yellow *n.* Lining from banana peels that is dried and smoked. It has been found to have no narcotic effect.

member *n.* (B) Member of the tribe; Black person.

mental hernia *n.* Seemingly ignorant person—eg. *That guy is really a mental hernia.*

meprobamate (me-prō'-bə-māt) *n.* (med) Minor tranquilizer that is used as a muscle relaxant and in the treatment of anxiety. It can be physically addictive. See EQUANIL; MILTOWN.

mesc *n.* (d) Mescaline. See MESCALINE.

mescaline *n.* (d) (3,4,5-trimethoxy-phenylethylamine) the hallucinogenic alkaloid that is derived from the buttons of the peyote cactus or is sometimes synthesized. It is similar to LSD but is less potent. Mescaline is swallowed, and the duration of its action is eight to 12 hours. It is not physically addictive, but psychological dependence may occur. **a.k.a.** the big chief, cactus, the chief, pumpkin seed, yellow football. See BUTTON; HALLUCINOGEN; PEYOTE.

mesmerizing eye *n.* (d) All-seeing eye of the LSD user.

Some of these people wear a symbolic dot on the center of the forehead.

mess around *v.* Do something just for the sake of doing it. **a.k.a.** goof, goof around, goof off.

mess up *v.* Make a mistake; spoil; ruin. **a.k.a.** fuck up, goof, goof up.

messed up *adj.* **1.** (d) Extremely high on drugs. See LOADED. **2.** Emotionally incompetent; unable to function. **3.** Ruined; made errors; spoiled.

meth n. (d) Methedrine, an amphetamine. See AMPHETAMINE; METHEDRINE.

meth freak *n.* Habitual user of Methedrine. See FREAK; METHEDRINE.

meth head *n.* (d) Methedrine addict. See HEAD; METHEDRINE.

methadone *n.* (med) (methadone hydrochloride) Synthetic narcotic used in treating heroin addiction. It eliminates heroin withdrawal symptoms; however, it is addicting in itself. Methadone is used extensively at Lexington. (See CURE, THE; LEXINGTON.) Its withdrawal symptoms are less severe but more prolonged than those of heroin or morphine. Methadone creates a physical and psychic dependence. **a.k.a.** dolly.

Methedrine (meth-ə-drēn') *n.* (med) (Methamphetamine; Burroughs, Wellcome & Company.) Methedrine creates a stimulating effect. It is often used by heroin addicts to avoid withdrawal pains and because it is less expensive and more accessible. **a.k.a.** bombita, meth, speed, zoom. See AMPHETAMINE.

methyl di-amphetamine *n.* (d) MDA, a stimulant. Called methamphetamine or methamp for short by dope users. See AMPHETAMINE.

Mexican brown *n.* (d) A grade of marijuana. See MARIJUANA.

Mexican green *n.* (d) A grade of marijuana. See MARIJUANA.

Mexican jumping bean *n.* (d) Seconal, manufactured

in Mexico and smuggled into the U.S. See SE-CONAL.
Mexican red (d) A grade of marijuana. See MARIJUANA.
michoacan (mi-chō-ah-kahn') *n.* Fine bright-green marijuana of very high quality. The name is derived from the state in Mexico where it originates.
Mickey Finn *n.* (d) Chloral hydrate; knockout drops. **a.k.a.** joy juice, peter. See CHLORAL HYDRATE.
mickey mouse *n.* Policeman. See POLICEMAN. *adj.* Phony, routine, simple.
micro- *adj.* Prefix meaning extremely small—eg. *microbopper* = very young aware person. See BOPPER.
mighty mezz, the *n.* (d) **1.** Marijuana. Named after Mezz Mezzrow, Black Harlem jazz musician of the 1930s and 40s. Mighty came from the fact that he rolled very large cigarettes (see BOMBER). See MARIJUANA. **2.** Marijuana cigarette. See MARIJUANA CIGARETTE.
mike *n.* (d) Microgram (millionth of a gram).
milk someone *v.* (pr) Find out if a person has a venereal disease (V.D.) by massaging the penis (before having intercourse) until fluid comes out. Prostitutes do this to prevent catching V.D. If a white viscous fluid appears at the tip, there is usually no V.D. If any other coloration appears, it implies some form of V.D.
milk sugar *n.* Crystals of lactose. Milk sugar resembles heroin in appearance and is used to dilute heroin to fool the buyer. See CUT.
millet seeds *n.* Small round seeds smoked to obtain a high. They are available in health-food stores.
Miltown *n.* (med) (meprobamate; Wallace Pharmaceuticals) A minor tranquilizer used in treatment of anxiety. See EQUANIL; MEPROBAMATE.
mind bender *n.* **1.** (d) Drug that expands the mind, eg., a hallucinogen. **2.** Person or event that expands the mind or increases one's knowledge or understanding.

mind blower *n.* Unusual experience; sudden shock. Can be while under the influence of drugs.

mind explorer *n.* (d) **1.** User of LSD. **a.k.a.** mind opener. **2.** Seller of LSD. **a.k.a.** mind opener.

mind fucker *n.* **1.** Individual who asserts personal pressure to persuade people to believe his way without regard for the feelings of the people he influences; person who attempts to manipulate another's thinking without consideration for the other. See PUT ONE'S TRIP. **2.** Thing or situation that upsets or disturbs one.

mind opener *n.* (d) **1.** User of LSD. **a.k.a.** mind explorer. **2.** Seller of LSD. **a.k.a.** mind explorer.

mind tripper *n.* (d) One who uses drugs for the resulting effect upon his states of consciousness. See TRIP.

mini- *adj.* Prefix meaning small—eg. *minibopper, miniskirt.* See BOPPER.

minstrel *n.* 12.5-mg. capsule of an amphetamine and a sedative. **a.k.a.** black and white, black and white minstrel, domino. See SPEEDBALL.

miss *v.* (d) Fail to hit a vein when injecting a drug. *n.* (d) An injection that fails to hit a vein.

miss emma *n.* Morphine. See MORPHINE.

Mister Charlie *n.* **1.** (B) White man; boss. **2.** White Establishment man. He is one who lives in suburbia, usually has a white-collar job, two to three children, a station wagon and a compact car, and a white picket fence. He has short hair and puts the American flag outside his house on patriotic holidays. In short, he is a part of mainstream American life and society. **a.k.a.** herbie, Mister Jones. See ESTABLISHMENT; WASP.

Mister Jones *n.* White Establishment man. **a.k.a.** herbie, Mister Charlie. See ESTABLISHMENT; MISTER CHARLIE.

mix your peanut butter *v.* (p) Have anal intercourse, a common activity in prison. Peanut butter probably refers to fecal matter (shit). **a.k.a.** get some round eye, ram.

M.J. *n.* (d) Marijuana. The initials stand for Mary Jane. See MARIJUANA.

moby grape *n.* (d) Syringe with a bulb on the end used for shooting drugs into a vein. The rubber bulb comes from a child's pacifier. See FIT.

mod squad *n.* (B) Interracial couple or group of people. Comes from TV show of the same name.

mohair *n.* Black female with hair in natural style. See NATURAL.

mojo (mō-jō) *n.* **1.** (B) Charm; amulet. Common use of the term in the Southern Black culture; appears in many songs. **2.** (d) Narcotics; morphine. See MORPHINE.

money *n.* **a.k.a.** blood bread, B.R., bread, brocas, cactus, coins, dough, dust, ends, fierro, ghedis, green, lace, lettuce, long green, red bread, scratch.

monkey *n.* (d) Drug habit. Usually said: Monkey on my back. Refers to heroin.

monkey bite *n.* Mark made on skin by sucking or biting. **a.k.a.** hickey.

monolithic *adj.* (d) Extremely high on a drug. See LOADED.

moocah *n.* (d) Marijuana. See MARIJUANA.

moon *n.* (d) Peyote. **a.k.a.** peyotl. See HALLUCINOGEN; PEYOTE.

moon, hit the See HIT THE MOON.

moon, reach for the See REACH FOR THE MOON.

morning-glory seed *n.* (d) Morning-glory seeds are used as a hallucinogen. They are crushed into a powder, soaked in water for a period of time and the juice is drunk, or they can be eaten in seed form, to obtain a high. Many North American Indians use morning-glory seeds in religious rites. Some effects are similar to LSD **a.k.a.** flying saucer, heavenly blue, pearly gate.

morph *n.* (d) Morphine. See MORPHINE.

morphine (mor'-fēn) *n.* (med) Morphine sulfate is a natural alkaloid of opium. It is even more addictive than opium. Morphine treated with acetic acid is equivalent to heroin except that it lacks the characteristic euphoric rush of heroin. It is similar to heroin, but is less potent. Morphine can be swallowed or injected; it is usually injected. Its duration of action is four hours. Morphine is medically used to relieve pain. Since morphine depresses respiration, a major hazard of the drug is respiratory failure. The body develops a tolerance to morphine within a few weeks. After that, very large doses can be taken. The physical and psychological effects of morphine are similar to those of heroin. **a.k.a.** aunt emma, cubes, dream, joy powder, M, mary, mary ann, miss emma, mojo, morph, pins and needles, white stuff.

moshky *n.* User of marijuana. **a.k.a.** motter, M.U., muggle head, muggles.

mota *n.* High-quality marijuana. See MARIJUANA.

mother *n.* **1.** Insult; derogatory name—eg. *You mother!* **a.k.a.** mother fucker. See FUCK; MOTHER FUCK. **2.** Positive, complimentary name for a friend. **a.k.a.** mother fucker. See MOTHER FUCK. **3.** Drug seller. See PUSHER.

mother fuck (B) **1.** Greeting to another person. It has a positive connotation. See MOTHER; MOTHER FUCKER. **2.** Negative connotation when used in anger to express hostility—eg. *You mother fuck!* See MOTHER; MOTHER FUCKER.

mother fucker *n.* **1.** Exclamation of anger. **2.** Insult; derogatory name; bastard. **a.k.a.** mother. See MOTHER FUCK. **3.** Positive, complimentary name for a friend—eg. *Hey, mother fucker, what's happening?* **a.k.a.** mother. See FUCK; MOTHER FUCK. **4.** Hard-to-solve problem; rough situation—eg. *What a mother fucker this is!*

NOTE: Dr. Charles G. Hurst, president of Malcolm X College in Chicago, has compiled twelve different connotations commonly used in the Black community for this word.

mother's day *n.* Day one gets one's welfare check. Most drug addicts are on welfare, especially female addicts who have children.

moths in one's pocket, have See HAVE MOTHS IN ONE'S POCKET.

motion, make a See MAKE A MOTION.

motter *n.* (d) User of marijuana. **a.k.a.** moshky, M.U., muggle head, muggles.

mouthpiece *n.* Lawyer.

move on out *v.* Commence activity; start.

move out *v.* Steal—eg. *See if you can move out a table and chairs for me.*

moxie *n.* Loud-mouth; "wise ass." **a.k.a.** moxy. **2.** Courage. **a.k.a.** moxy.

moxy See MOXIE.

Mr. Charlie See MISTER CHARLIE.

Mr. Jones See MISTER JONES.

M.U. *n.* (d) Marijuana user. **a.k.a.** moshky, motter, muggle head, muggles.

mucara (myōō-ka'-ra) *n.* (med) A laxative. Its active ingredient is karaya gum. Mucara can be bought without prescription. It is a way to obtain a small high.

mud *n.* (d) Opium. See OPIUM.

muggle *n.* (d) Marijuana cigarette. See MARIJUANA CIGARETTE.

muggle head *n.* (d) User of marijuana. **a.k.a.** moshky, motter, M.U., muggles. See HEAD.

muggles *n.* (d) User of marijuana. **a.k.a.** moshky, motter, M.U., muggle head.

mule *n.* (d) Person who sells or transports drugs for a regular seller (pusher).

munchies *n.* (d) Hunger induced by marijuana—eg. *I have the munchies.*

mungy *adj.* (d) Describes the state and feeling of having a very oily face when one is on an acid (LSD) trip—eg. *My face feels mungy.*

mushroom See PEYOTE.

mushroom, sacred See SACRED MUSHROOM.

mushroom chance *n.* Multitude of opportunities and/or alternatives—eg. *I've got a mushroom chance.*

mutha *n.* (d) Marijuana. See MARIJUANA.

my jaws are tight (B) Expression meaning I'm angry.

n

nab *n.* Policeman. See POLICEMAN.

nail *n.* (d) Hypodermic needle (used to inject drugs). See FIT.

nail (someone) *v.* **1.** Have sexual relations with. See COPULATE. **2.** Get back at; hit; kill. Old hoodlum term.

nailed *adj.* Found to be under the influence of a drug as determined by the Nalline test. See NALLINE TEST.

nail-polish remover *n.* Substance inhaled for a high.

Nalline *n.* (med) (nalorphine; Merck Sharp & Dohme) Semisynthetic derivative of morphine. It acts to reverse the effects of morphine and other opiates. It is physically addictive. Nalline is not used by drug takers to get high, but it is used in a test made by the police department to determine if a person is using drugs. See NALLINE TEST.

Nalline test *n.* (med) A test in which Nalline is injected into a vein to determine by the amount of dilation of the pupil of the eye whether or not a person is on or has been recently using opiates. See NALLINE.

narc *n.* (d) Narcotics officer. **a.k.a.** fuzz, narco, sam, wisher. See FED.

narco *n.* (d) Narcotics officer. **a.k.a.** fuzz, narc, sam, wisher. See FED.

narcotic *n.* (med) Drug that relieves pain and is physically addictive. Includes opium, morphine, codeine and their derivatives.

natch, on the See ON THE NATCH.

natural *n.* Natural Black hair style; hair not straightened but left curly. **a.k.a.** Afro. See PROCESS.

natural speed See GINSENG.

natural trip *n.* (d) High obtained from legal substances, eg., catnip, millet seed. **a.k.a.** legal high.

nebbie *n.* (d) Nembutal. See BARBITURATE; NEMBUTAL.

neck *v.* Kiss and caress from the neck up. **a.k.a.** make out.

needle *n.* (d) Hypodermic needle or substitute used for injection of a drug.

needle, on the See ON THE NEEDLE.

needle candy *n.* (d) Any narcotic taken by injection.

needle man *n.* (d) Addict who injects drugs.

nel (*Spanish*) Expression meaning no. **a.k.a.** chale.

nellie fag *n.* (h) Homosexual male who is the epitome of effeminate appearance in walk, gestures and speech. See HOMOSEXUAL.

Nembutal (nem'-byo͞o-təl) *n.* (med) (pentobarbital; Abbott Laboratories) A barbiturate. It is medically used as a hypnotic in treatment of insomnia and as a sedative in a wide variety of other conditions. **a.k.a.** abbott, nebbie, nemish, nemmie, nimby, yellow, yellow jacket. See BARBITURATE.

nemish *n.* (d) Nembutal. See BARBITURATE; NEMBUTAL.

nemmie *n.* (d) Nembutal. See BARBITURATE; NEMBUTAL.

New York tuck and roll See TUCK AND ROLL.

nicked *adj.* (p) Arrested.

nickel *n.* **1.** (d) Five dollars. **2.** (p) Five-year prison sentence.

nickel bag *n.* (d) Five-dollar bag of any drug. **a.k.a.** Five-cent paper, five-dollar bag. See QUANTITIES OF DRUGS.

nimby *n.* (d) Nembutal. See BARBITURATE; NEMBUTAL.

ninny jug *n.* (B) Female's breast. See BREAST.

nitty gritty *n.* Basic or real situation; the core of a problem—eg. *Let's get down to the real nitty gritty.* **a.k.a.** where it's at.

no chance Expression meaning refusal to be persuaded to do something. **a.k.a.** no way.

no sweat Expression meaning (1) don't worry or (2) that something will be effortless; easy—eg. *That test was no sweat.*

no way Expression meaning refusal to be persuaded to do something. **a.k.a.** no chance.

no-art *n.* Term applied to psychedelic art. Called no-art because by accepted standards it is not considered art. See PSYCHEDELIC.

nod *n.* (d) Motion made by the head, shoulders and body that is similar to that of drowsiness or semiconsciousness. This condition, known as nodding, is common among drug addicts (heroin) and barbiturate users but is uncommon among amphetamine users. See FALL OUT; ON THE NOD.

nod, on the See ON THE NOD.

nookie *n.* **1.** Vagina. See VAGINA. **2.** Sexual intercourse —eg. *I want some nookie.* See COPULATION.

nowhere *adj.* Describes a person who is not very knowledgeable or "in" or who has not achieved a position of status; describes a situation that is meaningless or boring.

number *n.* **1.** (d) Marijuana cigarette. See MARIJUANA CIGARETTE. **2.** Unusual occurrence; something different—eg. *They really put me through a number.* **3.** Event; job; something to do—eg. *I can't do that number.* **4.** Psychological game.

nurd *n.* Individual lacking in social grace; jerk; dumb person.

nut *v.* Have sexual intercourse—eg. *Did you nut her?* See COPULATE.

nutmeg *n.* Substance used to get high. Two teaspoons are swallowed straight. This high lasts for only a few minutes.

nuts *n.* Testicles. See GET ONE'S NUTS OFF; LOVE NUTS; TESTICLES.

O

O *n.* (d) Opium. See OPIUM.

O.D. *v.* Use enough drugs to display the symptoms of an overdose—eg. *He O.D.ed last night.* *n.* (d) Overdose. Used by hospitals, police and drug users to describe the state of having taken too much of a drug. Can be enough to cause death. **a.k.a.** overjolt.

ódale (*Spanish* o'-dah-lā) Expression meaning (1) yes, I agree; (2) let's go; (3) all right; right on! **a.k.a.** ándale.

ofay *n.* (B) Derogatory term for a white person. **a.k.a.** fay, peckawood.

off artist *n.* Thief.

off the top Describes first thing that comes to your mind.

off the wall Surprising; unusual—eg. *That statement from you is really off the wall.*

old lady *n.* **1.** Wife. See WIFE. **2.** Girl friend. See GIRL FRIEND. **3.** Woman a man lives with. **4.** Mother.

on *n.* Indebtedness to someone—eg. *I have an on to him* = I owe him a favor. *adj.* (d) **1.** High on a drug. See LOADED. **2.** Using drugs.

on the beam *adj.* Feeling fine.

on the case discussing a person's personal problem.

on the natch 1. (d) Get off a drug without taking another drug to ease the pain. See COLD TURKEY; WITHDRAWAL. **2.** Do something without aid or assistance.

on the needle (d) Injecting drugs.

on the nod Describes drowsiness resulting from drug use. See FALL OUT; NOD.

on the outs 1. Angry at; not talking to—eg. *I'm on the outs with John.* **2.** Outside of a prison, hospital, home or any institution—eg. *When I get on the outs, I'm going to get me a big steak.*

on the rag On the menstrual cycle. **a.k.a.** O.T.R.

on the road Expression meaning living a nomadic life; traveling about with all one's belongings; "sleeping rough"; bedding down with others. **a.k.a.** skip. See CRASH PAD; SKIPPER; SLEEP ROUGH.

on the rod (d) Taking another drug after injecting heroin.

on the run 1. Moving around to different cities; nomadic. **2.** Moving around to avoid detection by parents or police, eg., a runaway teen-ager.

on the shelf (p) in solitary confinement in prison. **a.k.a.** in the hole.

on the street 1. (p) Out of jail. **2.** Free; not working or going to school; hanging around on the streets. **3.** In search of, eg., a homosexual looking for action, a guy looking for a girl, a doper looking for drugs.

on to, be See BE ON TO.

ones and twos *n*. (p) Shoes.

op (ōp) *n*. (d) Opium. See OPIUM.

opium *n*. (med) Narcotic from which morphine, codeine and heroin are derived. Opium is medically used for relief of severe pain and treatment of gastrointestinal disorders. The white milky substance is extracted from the unripe seed pods of a poppy (*Papaver somniferum*). This is dried and forms a brown gummy mass that is heated to convert it for smoking. Drug users use opium to obtain a heroin- or barbiturate-type high. Opium is highly addictive. The physical dependence is very long lasting and the withdrawal symptoms are very painful (see WITHDRAWAL). Opium is smoked heavily in China, Hong Kong and Southeast Asia. The smoker usually smokes it lying down on his side in order to lessen the nausea it produces. **a.k.a.** black stuff, can, Chinese tobacco, cubes, dream, gunji, ice cream, mud, O, op, pen yuen, tar.

O.R. (p) Own recognizance. When arrested, sometimes the individual will be released on his own recognizance to return for court hearing; this means he doesn't have to put up bail.

oral copulation *v.* Kiss, lick, suck the genital area of another. **a.k.a.** blow, do, eat, eat out, flip flop, give head, go down on, gum it, scarf, 69, spoon, talk to the canoe driver, tongue. *n.* Act of kissing, licking, sucking the genital area of another. **a.k.a.** blow job, cunnilingus, fellatio, head, head job, hum job, loop-de-loop, pipe job, skull job. See BLOWHOLE.

orange *n.* (d) **1.** Orange-colored tablet of LSD usually mixed with methamphetamines. **a.k.a.** sunshine, yellow. **2.** Dexedrine tablet.

orange wedge *n.* (d) Combination of acid (LSD) and speed (Methedrine) in one pill. **a.k.a.** peace pill.

originals *n.* Levi's that have never been washed. (Levi's is a brand name of blue jeans.)

O.T.R. *n.* On the rag; on the menstrual cycle.

out front *adj.* Open; honest; not lying.

out of body (d) Feeling of being outside of oneself while under LSD; feeling that you stand aside from yourself and see yourself.

out of it *adj.* **1.** Unaware; unknowing generally; not in tune with the times. **a.k.a.** out to lunch. **2.** Unable to function. **3.** (d) High on a drug. See LOADED.

out of one's mind *adj.* **1.** (d) Under the influence of drugs or alcohol. See LOADED. **2.** Crazy. **a.k.a.** out to lunch.

out of one's tree Expression meaning (1) be thinking, talking or acting in an irrational way—eg. *You are talking out of your tree* or (2) be in an unfamiliar place.

out of shape *adj.* Disturbed; angry; irrational. **a.k.a** bent, bent out of shape, pushed out of shape.

out of sight *adj.* Great; wonderful; marvelous; fantastic—eg. *That movie was out of sight!* See GROOVY.

out to lunch *adj.* **1.** Unaware of the things happening around one. **a.k.a.** out of it. **2.** Crazy. **a.k.a.** out of one's mind. **3.** Having sexual intercourse.

outfit *n.* Equipment used for preparing and injecting drugs. See FIT.

outs, on the See ON THE OUTS.

oven cleaner *n.* Substance used to get high. It is sprayed into a bag and inhaled.

overamp (ō'-vər-amp) *n.* (d) Hallucinating state induced by an overdose of Methedrine. The heart becomes overstimulated and blood pressure rises. The person becomes lightheaded and extremely uncomfortable and may lose consciousness.

overdose *n.* (med) State of having taken too much of a drug. It can result in death. **a.k.a.** O.D., overjolt.

overjolt *n.* (d) Overdose (of a drug). **a.k.a.** O.D.

overseer *n.* **1.** Person who takes a mother role. **2.** (B) Mother—eg. *I've got to call my overseer and tell her something.*

owsley (ahz'-lē) *n.* (d) Highest-quality LSD. Named after Augustus Owsley. See OWSLEY, AUGUSTUS.

Owsley, Augustus. Grandson of a senator from Kentucky. Known for his illegal manufacture of high-potency LSD.

O.Z. *n.* (d) An ounce (of a drug). See QUANTITIES OF DRUGS.

p

pachuca (*Spanish* pah-choo-kah) See PACHUCO.

pachuco (*Spanish* pah-choo'-kō) *n.* Mexican-American young person, usually rowdy, tough, sometimes a member of a gang. They dress and wear their hair in certain styles. **a.k.a.** cholo.

pack up *v.* Leave. See LEAVE.

packet *n.* (d) Piece of paper rolled tightly in a funnel-shaped form and packed with a drug; the top is folded over to secure the drug. This is the usual method in which a powdered drug is carried. See BAG; QUANTITIES OF DRUGS.

pad *n.* Home; house or apartment. See HOME.

paddy *n.* White person. Term used by Mexican-Americans and Blacks. See GRINGO.

paint *n.* Substance sniffed to obtain a high.

pale face *n.* (B) White person. See GRINGO.

pan up *v.* (d) Put a drug in the implement used to cook it; liquefy a drug for injection. **a.k.a.** cook, cook up.

Panama *n.* (d) Marijuana. Comes from Panama gold. See MARIJUANA; PANAMA GOLD.

Panama gold *n.* (d) High-quality marijuana grown in Panama. More potent than Panama red. See ACAPULCO GOLD; MARIJUANA.

Panama red *n.* (d) Marijuana grown in Panama. More potent than U.S. marijuana. **a.k.a.** P.R., red. See MARIJUANA.

panic *n.* (d) Scarcity of drugs on the market. See HASSLE.

paper *n.* (d) Small packet containing a drug. See BAG.

paranoia *n.* All-pervasive fear of anything without reason to fear.

paregoric *n.* (med) Tincture of opium and camphor. It can be used to obtain a high. Paregoric is medically used for stomach disorders. **a.k.a.** P.G.

partner *n.* Very close friend; one who is with you regardless of what you do; person who will do anything with you and for you. Partner has almost completely replaced the word "friend" in the underground vocabulary.

pass Expression meaning (1) one has no thought on something or (2) inclination not to be involved.

pass for white Expression applied to a Black person who looks white and lives in the white world without detection of his Black heritage.

pattern *n.* (d) Hallucination. Described as time in motion. Usually occurs when using a drug. **a.k.a.** cartoon, trail.

patty *n.* White person. Commonly used by Mexican-Americans and Blacks. See GRINGO.

pava (*Spanish* pah'-vah) *n.* Act of ditching school. Used in the expression *hacer la pava*. **a.k.a.** pinta.

pawn *v.* Obtain a loan on an object. **a.k.a.** hock.

P.B. *n.* Poor bastard. **a.k.a.** fool, sucker.

PCP *n.* (d) Para-phenathrene. It is commonly used as a tranquilizer for animals in veterinary medicine. PCP comes in liquid and powder forms, and is used by young people to obtain a high. The known effects on humans are feelings of body transformation, spacelessness, and loss of the senses of time and motion. **a.k.a.** angel dust, fairy dust, hog, moon dust.

P.D. *n.* (d) See Seconal.

P.D.R. *n.* (med) *Physicians' Desk Reference*, a pharmacopoeia. **a.k.a.** the book. See PHYSICIANS' DESK REFERENCE.

peace Salutation used when meeting and parting. It has replaced hello and good-by to a considerable extent. The sign is made by holding forefinger and middle finger up in a V with the nails facing yourself. The written symbol is ☮ . Peace and love are ideas flower children pattern their lives on. See FLOWER; FLOWER CHILDREN.

peace pill *n.* (d) Mixture of LSD and Methedrine. **a.k.a.** orange wedge.

peace tab *n.* (d) Psilocybin, a hallucinogen similar to LSD. Tab is short for tablet. See HALLUCINOGEN; PSILOCYBIN.

peach *n.* (d) Amphetamine; an upper. See AMPHETAMINE.

peak *v.* (d) Reach the highest part of your drug trip. **a.k.a.** hit the moon. See REACH FOR THE MOON; THERE. *n.* That part of an LSD experience when you obtain the apex of sensory awareness, the highest part of the trip.

peanut *n.* (d) Barbiturate. See BARBITURATE.

peanut butter *n.* Peanut butter is being melted down and injected by young kids. There is no known high effect. It has been known to cause death.

peanut butter, mix your See MIX YOUR PEANUT BUTTER.

pearls *n.* (d) Amyl nitrite. See AMYL NITRITE.

pearly gate See MORNING-GLORY SEED.

peck *v.* (B) Eat. **a.k.a.** grease.

peckawood *n.* (B) White person. **a.k.a.** fay, ofay.

pecker *n.* Penis. See PENIS.

peddler *n.* (d) One who sells drugs. See PUSHER.

pee hole *n.* Vagina. See VAGINA.

pellet *n.* (d) **1.** Tablet. **2.** LSD capsule. **a.k.a.** tab.

pen yuen *n.* (d) Opium. See OPIUM.

pendejo (*Spanish* pen-dā'-hō) *n.* **1.** Stupid person. **2.** Very hostile insult. Literal translation: pubic hairs.

penis *n.* Male sex organ. **a.k.a.** bell rope, bone, cock, dick, dong, johnson, joint, lizard, meat, pecker, peter, phallus, prick, pud, putz, rod, schlong, schmuck, short arm, thing, tool, unit, whang.

peo (*Spanish* pe'-ō). *n.* Fart. See FART. *adj.* Drunk.

people *n.* Relatives; family; parents—eg. *How are your people?*

people farm *n.* **1.** Modern, fast-moving large city. **2.** Psychiatric institution. **3.** Home for the aged.

pep pill *n.* (d) **1.** Amphetamine. **2.** Dexedrine. **3.** Benzedrine. See AMPHETAMINE; BENZEDRINE; DEXEDRINE.

per *n.* (d) Prescription. **a.k.a.** reader, script.

Percobarb *n.* (med) (oxycodone hydrochloride and hexobarbital; Endo Laboratories) A synthetic derivative of morphine in combination with a barbiturate. It is medically used in cases of sleeplessness that are precipitated by pain. Percobarb has a sedative and analgesic effect. It is used by dopers to obtain a morphinelike high. Physical dependence can result from overuse, and withdrawal symptoms are similar to those of morphine.

Percodan *n.* (med) (oxycodone hydrochloride; Endo Laboratories) A synthetic derivative of morphine used for its analgesic properties. It is similar to Percobarb but has no barbiturate. Percodan is especially popular with heroin addicts. See PERCOBARB.

periwinkle leaves *n.* Substance used to get high. The leaves are dried, shredded and smoked.

peter *n.* **1.** Penis. See PENIS **2.** (d) Chloral hydrate. **a.k.a.** joy juice, Mickey Finn. See CHLORAL HYDRATE.

peyote (pā-ō'-tē) *n.* A small cactus (*Lophophora williamsii*). The main alkaloid in peyote is mescaline. It causes hallucinations and is used by many North and South American Indian tribes in religious rites. The spineless heads of the plant (buttons), which resemble mushrooms, are cut off and dried; then they are chewed or boiled and the water is drunk. The taste is very bitter and nausea usually accompanies ingestion. There is no physical addiction and no withdrawal symptoms, but psychic dependence may occur. **a.k.a.** moon, peyotl. See BUTTON; HALLUCINOGEN; MESCALINE; TOP.

peyotl *n.* (d) Peyote. A Nahuatl Indian (Mexico) word. See PEYOTE.

P.G. *n.* (d) Paregoric. See PAREGORIC.

phallus *n.* Penis. See PENIS.

phenie *n.* (d) Barbiturate. See BARBITURATE.

pheno *n* (d) User of phenobarbital.

phenobarbital (fē-nō-bahr'-bi-təl) *n.* (med) A crystalline compound used medically as a hypnotic in insomnia and states of nervous excitement and as a sedative in epilepsy. Its effect is similar to a barbiturate.

phony *n.* Person who makes obscene phone calls. Comes from phone, telephone.

physical dependence (on a drug) *n.* (d) State that results when a person is addicted to a drug. That is, if he does not receive a sufficient dose, he will experience withdrawal symptoms. The drugs that produce physical dependence are opiates, barbiturates and alcohol. See WITHDRAWAL.

Physicians' Desk Reference *n.* Pharmacopoeia, a reference for drug information. The *Physicians' Desk Reference* contains a list by chemical name, brand name and company of all drugs produced, complete with color pictures of various pills for identification and classification purposes. It also contains lists of uses, indications, counterindications, doses and all other medical information. The P.D.R., as it is affectionately referred to, is used by physicians commonly and by their counter colleagues, the addicts, for this information. **a.k.a.** the book, P.D.R.

pick up *v.* **1.** Obtain drugs from a dealer. **2.** Develop some form of relationship with a member of the opposite sex without introduction. **3.** Arrest. **4.** (d) Light up a marijuana cigarette. See MARIJUANA CIGARETTE. *n.* **1.** Person who can be picked up without introduction. **2.** (d) Drugs waiting to be obtained from the dealer.

picker *n.* Person who enjoys watching other people involved in sexual or private activities; peeping Tom. The watcher usually feels sexual enjoyment from watching. **a.k.a.** voyeur.

piece *n.* **1.** Sexual intercourse—eg. *I got a good piece last night.* See COPULATION. **2.** One ounce of her-

piece of ass

oin. See QUANTITIES OF DRUGS. **3.** Hand gun. See HEAT. **4.** (B) Girl friend; wife. See GIRL FRIEND; WIFE.

piece of ass *n.* Sexual intercourse. See COPULATION.

piece of tail *n.* Sexual intercourse. See COPULATION

pig *n.* Policeman. See POLICEMAN.

pile *v.* (B) Have sexual intercourse. See COPULATE.

pill *n.* Any drug in pill form.

pill, the Oral contraceptive. See CONTRACEPTIVE.

pill head *n.* (d) Habitual user of amphetamines or barbiturates. See AMPHETAMINE; BARBITURATE; HEAD.

pill party *n.* (p) In the state of California, a legal means of execution (capital punishment) is the gas chamber. The gas is released when two pills of cyanide fall into a pail of water beneath the victim, giving off the deadly fumes. It is from these pills that this type of execution became known as a pill party.

pimp *v.* Procure clients for a prostitute. **a.k.a.** mack. *n.* (pr) Person who procures clients for the prostitute or a group of prostitutes and takes a percentage of their income.

pin *v.* **1.** Identify an individual or his style of life or a particular aspect about him—eg. *I pinned him as a homosexual.* **2.** Catch someone doing something and blame him for it; finger. **3.** Stare at someone or something. *n.* (d) Very small marijuana cigarette. See MARIJUANA CIGARETTE.

pin head *n.* **1.** (d) User of amphetamines. See AMPHETAMINE; HEAD. **2.** Small-minded person.

pin point *adj.* Refers to the contraction of the pupils of the eyes during a drug experience. **a.k.a.** pinned.

pink *n.* LSD. See HALLUCINOGEN; LYSERGIC ACID DIETHYLAMIDE. **2.** Seconal capsule. See BARBITURATE; SECONAL.

pink lemonade *n.* (d) Cleaning fluid injected into a vein. Often used by Methedrine addicts. It can cause death.

pink swirl *n.* (d) LSD. See HALLUCINOGEN; LYSERGIC ACID DIETHYLAMIDE.

pinkie *n.* (B) White person.

pinned *adj.* (d) Constricted state of the pupils of the eyes due to use of drugs. **a.k.a.** pin point.

pins and needles *n.* (d) Morphine. See MORPHINE.

pinta (*Spanish* pēn'-tah) *n.* **1.** Act of ditching school. Used in the expression *hacer la pinta*. **a.k.a.** pava. **2.** Jail. See CLINK.

pipe *n.* (d) **1.** Person who uses marijuana. **2.** Pipe used to smoke marijuana. See HOOKAH.

pipe, take the See TAKE THE PIPE.

pipe job *n.* Oral copulation by the female to the male. **a.k.a.** blow job, fellatio. See ORAL COPULATION.

piss *v.* Urinate *n.* **1.** Urine. **2.** Exclamation of disgust —eg. *Oh, piss!* See PISSED.

pissed *adj.* Very angry. **a.k.a.** hacked, hacked off, pissed at, pissed off (at).

pissed at *adj.* Very angry. **a.k.a.** hacked, hacked off, pissed, pissed off (at).

pissed off (at) *adj.* Very angry. **a.k.a.** hacked, hacked off, pissed, pissed at.

pit *n.* (d) The large vein that leads to the heart.

pitch *n.* (h, p) Aggressor or male role of a homosexual relationship; the male role in anal intercourse or oral copulation. Used in the expression pitch and catch. See CATCH.

place *n.* The part of an LSD trip when one reaches the point of total awareness.

Placidyl *n.* (med) (ethchlorvynol; Abbott Laboratories) A non-barbiturate hypnotic used for treating anxiety.

plant *v.* **1.** (p) Place drugs on the person or on the premises of a suspected drug user or seller to facilitate an arrest and conviction. **a.k.a.** set up. **2.** (d) Hide something. *n.* That which is planted on a person or is hidden. Usually refers to drugs.

plastic *adj.* Phony; unreal; dehumanized; superficial; valueless. From concept that plastic is synthetic, not natural. Also refers to practice of mass production and concern for material objects—eg. *We live in a plastic society* or *The inhabitants of that neighborhood are such plastic people.*

plastic hippy *n.* One who infrequently assumes the role of a hippy for status purposes or seeks hippy-like situations without in reality having any commitment to the hippy way of life; a pseudo hippy or hippy hypocrite.

player *n.* (d) **1.** Person who takes drugs. **2.** Seller of drugs. See PUSHER.

pleasure smoker *n.* One who smokes marijuana only occasionally. See CHIPPY.

P.O. *n.* (p) Probation officer; parole officer.

po' boy *n.* (B) Welfare check.

pocha (*Spanish* pō'-cha) See POCHO.

pocho (*Spanish* pō'-chō) *n.* **1.** Person who speaks English and Spanish mixed together. **2.** A Mexican-American. Term used by Mexicans who live in Mexico. *adj.* **1.** Describes a person who speaks a mixture of Spanish and English. **2.** Mexican-American.

pod *n.* (d) Marijuana. See MARIJUANA.

point *n.* (d) Needle used for injections. See FIT.

poison *n.* (d) Heroin. It is called poison because it is the most destructive of the addictive drugs. See HEROIN.

poison people *n.* (d) Heroin addicts.

police *n.* **a.k.a.** heat.

policeman *n.* **a.k.a.** azul, big John, bim, black and white, blue boy, boy scout, bull, chota, cop, do gooder, fuzz, Irvine, the man, mickey mouse, nab, pig, Tasmanian pig, tombo.

poopkie (pōōp'-kē) (d) Pipe for smoking marijuana. See HOOKAH.

pop *v.* (d) Inject a drug under the skin, intramuscularly or subcutaneously, not into a vein. **a.k.a.** skin pop. See MAINLINE. *n.* Intramuscular injection. **a.k.a.** job off, skin, skin pop.

pop party *n.* (d) A party where people inject drugs together.

popped *adj.* Arrested or picked up for questioning.

popper *n.* (d) Amyl nitrite. See AMYL NITRITE.

popsie *n.* (d) Amyl nitrite. See AMYL NITRITE.

porridge *n.* (p) Prison sentence.

pot *n.* Marijuana. Pot and grass are the most common terms for marijuana. MARIJUANA.

pot luck *n.* (d) Any drug one has around. People sometimes get together and combine all their drugs and take whatever is there—eg. *I'll take pot luck.*

pot party *n.* A party where people smoke pot (marijuana). **a.k.a.** blast party, blasting party.

pothead *n.* (d) Habitual heavy user of marijuana. **a.k.a.** gangster. See HEAD.

potsville *n.* (d) Use of marijuana. Comes from pot, which means marijuana.

pound *n.* (d) One pound of marijuana. See QUANTITIES OF DRUGS.

pound cotton *v.* (d) Pour water from eyedropper on old used cotton to draw out the drug left in it. See COTTON; COTTON HEAD; COTTON TOP.

power, in See IN POWER.

P.R. *n.* **1.** (d) Panama red, a type of marijuana. **a.k.a.** red. See MARIJUANA; PANAMA RED. **2.** Derogatory term for a Puerto Rican.

press someone's buttons *v.* **1.** Verbally make another angry or disturbed; antagonize. **a.k.a.** push someone's buttons. **2.** Act mechanically; appear computerized, as if someone were pressing your buttons. **a.k.a.** push someone's buttons.

pretty boy *n.* Someone overly concerned with his appearance, very conceited.

prick *n.* **1.** Penis. See PENIS. **2.** Obnoxious male.

prick teaser *n.* Female who acts as if she wants to engage in sexual intercourse but in reality doesn't; a tease. **a.k.a.** P.T.

Prince Albert can *n.* (d) Tobacco can used as a quantity for measuring drugs. See QUANTITIES OF DRUGS.

process *n.* (B) Hair style that used to be popular

among Black people. The hair is straightened with a hot comb and chemicals. With the rise of Black pride, the process was abandoned in favor of the natural. See AFRO; NATURAL.

prostitute *n.* **a.k.a.** bat, hooker, hustler, puta, scuffer, slut, whore, working girl.

psilocybin (si-lə-sī′ bin) *n.* (med) (3 (2 dimethylamino) ethylindo-4-01-dihydrogen phosphate) Hallucinogen similar to LSD. It is swallowed and its duration of action is six to eight hours. Initial reactions of nausea, muscular relaxation and headaches are followed by visual and auditory hallucinations. It is also found as an alkaloid in certain mushrooms. **a.k.a.** peace tabs. See HALLUCINOGEN; MAGIC MUSHROOM; SACRED MUSHROOM.

psych *n.* Psychologist or psychiatrist. **a.k.a.** head shrinker, shrink.

psych out *v.* **1.** Figure out. **2.** Disturb; upset—eg. *That movie really psyched me out.*

psyched out *adj.* Incapable of thinking rationally.

psyched up *adj.* Excited; anticipating something.

psychedelia *n.* (d) Those items that are associated with the use of psychedelic drugs. See PSYCHEDELIC.

psychedelic *adj.* Original meaning was consciousness-expanding sensory experiences. Now refers to a new social movement including the change in moral structure, music, dress and the arts.

psychedelic art *n.* Art that is associated with psychedelic drugs due to its ability to evoke consciousness-expanding states of perception. It evokes or imitates the experience of taking psychedelic drugs. See PSYCHEDELIC.

psychedelic peanut (d) Peanut skins that are crushed and smoked. This practice is said to produce hallucinations.

psychedelphia *n.* San Francisco, especially the Haight-Ashbury area. See HAIGHT-ASHBURY.

psychic dependence (on a drug) *n.* Psychological need experienced after continued use of a drug. It is a strong desire for the pleasurable sensations produced by a drug, like hallucinations, elation and relief from reality without the drug. If a person who is psychologically dependent on a drug stops taking it, he may become very depressed and even have a psychotic reaction that he had previously suppressed with the use of the drug. Some drugs that are not physically addictive but often produce psychological dependence are the amphetamines, cocaine, LSD, marijuana, morning-glory seeds.

psychoactive *adj.* Describes the changes in perception and consciousness caused by a drug.

P.T. *n.* Prick teaser; female who gives the impression of being desirous of sexual intercourse but in reality has no intention of it; female who leads men on; a tease—eg. *She's a real P.T.*

P.T.A. *n.* Pussy, tits and ass: a quick female bath (a sponge bath). The washing of the pubic area, breasts and ass. Sometimes referred to as a P.T.A. bath. Not to be confused with Parent-Teacher Association.

pud *n.* Penis. See PENIS.

pull a train *v.* (m) Engage in sexual intercourse (a female) with male members of a gang one after another. See GANG BANG; MAMA.

pull the covers *v.* **1.** Tell another's secret. **2.** Uncover an unknown fact about someone.

pumpkin seed *n.* (d) Football-shaped, yellow tablet of mescaline. **a.k.a.** yellow football. See MESCALINE.

pump up *v.* (d) Clench and unclench one's fist in a pumplike action in order to make a vein in one's arm rise to facilitate injection. The arm is also tied off (a tie is placed around the forearm) to make the blood remain in the lower arm. See SELF-INJECTION POSITION; TIE OFF; TIE UP.

punch *v.* Have sexual intercourse. See COPULATE.

punk *n.* **1.** Weak, scared person; coward. **2.** (p) Homosexual. See HOMOSEXUAL. **3.** One who usually retaliates in an underhanded manner.

pure *adj.* (d) Undiluted; uncut (drug). See CUT.

purple *n.* LSD. See HALLUCINOGEN; LYSERGIC ACID DIETHYLAMIDE.

purple flat *n.* (d) LSD See HALLUCINOGEN; LYSERGIC ACID DIETHYLAMIDE.

purple heart *n.* Out-of-date term still used by the press and courts for a Dexamyl pill, a combination of Dexedrine and amobarbital (amphetamine and barbiturate). Comes from the color and shape of the pill. See DEXAMYL; SPEEDBALL.

push *v.* (d) Sell drugs. See PUSHER.

push someone's buttons See PRESS SOMEONE'S BUTTONS.

pushed *adj.* **1.** In the know. **2.** Expression meaning I know; knowledge of a specific thing—eg. *"Hey, you've got to go to work." "I'm pushed, man."*

pushed out *adj.* Drunk.

pushed out of shape *adj.* Angry. **a.k.a.** bent, bent out of shape, out of shape.

pusher *n.* (d) Person who sells narcotics. **a.k.a.** arreador, bagman, candy man, dealer, junker, mother, peddler, player, source, tambourine man, thoroughbred, trafficker, travel agent.

pussy *n.* **1.** Vagina. See VAGINA. **2.** Derogatory term for an overly passive male.

pussy cat *n.* Female. See FEMALE.

put down *v.* **1.** (d) Stop taking drugs. **2.** Insult another. **3.** Talk about something to someone—eg. *I don't like what you're putting down.* **4.** Criticize negatively. **a.k.a.** down. *n.* Insult; derogatory remark.

put on *v.* **1.** Create a façade, a false impression; fool someone; lie. **2.** Introduce another to a drug. **a.k.a.** turn on. *n.* **1.** False impression; façade; lie. **a.k.a.** flam, front, scam. **2.** Joke; subterfuge.

put one's trip *v.* (d) Attempt to convince another that what one believes is more important or significant—eg. *She wants to put her trip on me.* See MIND FUCKER.

put out first *v.* (d) Pay for drugs in advance and take delivery at a later date.

put someone through changes *v.* Surprise; affect a person by doing or saying something unexpected or that makes him really think. See CHANGES; GO THROUGH CHANGES.

put the make on *v.* Flirt with; try to have a sexual relation with. **a.k.a.** put the moves on. See MAKE.

put the moves on *v.* Flirt with; try to have a sexual relation with. **a.k.a.** put the make on. See MAKE.

put up *v.* (d) Put powdered drugs into capsules.

puta (*Spanish* po͞o'-tah) *n.* Whore. See PROSTITUTE.

putz *n.* Penis. See PENIS.

q

quail *n.* Female. See FEMALE.

quantities of drugs B, bag, bee, can, deck, dime bag, eighth, five-cent paper, five-dollar bag, fix, geezer, ½ can, half can, half piece, kee, key, ki, kite, lid, matchbox, nickel bag, O.Z., packet, piece, pound, Prince Albert can, quarter bag, sixteenth, smudge, spoon, tael, 10¢ bag, ten-cent bag, toxy, trey. See individual entries.

quarter *n.* (d) Twenty-five dollars.

quarter bag *n.* (d) Twenty-five dollars' worth of a drug. See BAG; QUANTITIES OF DRUGS.

queen *n.* (h) Male homosexual who plays the female role in a relationship. See HOMOSEXUAL.

queer *n., adj.* Homosexual. See HOMOSEXUAL.

quickie *n.* Sexual intercourse with a very fast climax.

quill *n.* (d) Folded matchbox cover or paper soda straw used for sniffing narcotics through the nose.

quim *n.* Vagina. See VAGINA.

quinine *n.* Used to dilute (cut) heroin. Used mainly because its bitter taste resembles the taste of heroin.

quit, won't See WON'T QUIT.

rag, on the See ON THE RAG.
rainbow *v.* (B) Have interracial sex or relationship. *n.* (d) Tuinal; a barbiturate. A strong hypnotic. See BARBITURATE; TUINAL.
rainy day woman *n.* (d) Marijuana. See MARIJUANA.
ralph *v.* Vomit. See VOMIT.
ram *v.* Have anal intercourse. **a.k.a.** get some round eye, mix your peanut butter.
ram job *n.* Anal intercourse.
rama (*Spanish* rah'-mah) *n.* Marijuana. See MARIJUANA.
rank *adj.* **1.** Foul smelling. **2.** Impolite; disagreeable.
rap *v.* **1.** Talk. **a.k.a.** blow. **2.** Talk randomly. **3.** (d) Talk compulsively while high on drugs. **4.** Degrade; "knock." *n.* A talk, conversation.
rare *v.* Inhale heroin or cocaine.
rat *n.* (p) Informer.
rate up *n.* One's own self-confidence or that received by praise—eg. *When she told me how I impressed her, it was a real rate up.*
raw jaw *n.* (d) Act of stealing narcotics from a pusher or user.
R.D. *n.* (d) Red devil. Seconal; a barbiturate. See BARBITURATE; SECONAL.
reach for the moon *v.* (d) Move toward the highest level of a drug trip. The higher one feels the closer one is to the moon, which is the highest point. From this expression the word "spaced" originated. See HIT THE MOON; PEAK; SPACED.
read *v.* Analyze; understand—eg. *I don't read you very well.*
reader *n.* (d) Prescription for drugs. **a.k.a.** per, script.
really 1 Term of agreement—eg. *"What a drag the cops are." "Really!"* **2.** Exclamation of indignation.
ream *v.* Orally copulate the anus. **a.k.a.** rim.

ream job *n.* Oral copulation of the anus with stimulation by the tongue. **a.k.a.** brown job, rim job. See DINGLE BERRY.

red *n.* (d) **1.** Panama red, a type of marijuana. **a.k.a.** P.R. See MARIJUANA; PANAMA RED. **2.** Seconal; a barbiturate. See BARBITURATE; SECONAL.

red and blue *n.* (d) Tuinal; a barbiturate. Comes from the color. See BARBITURATE; TUINAL.

red bird *n.* Seconal; a barbiturate. Comes from the color. See BARBITURATE; SECONAL.

red bread *n.* Money. Comes from blood bread, which is money obtained by selling one's blood (to buy drugs). See BLOOD BREAD; MONEY.

red devil *n.* (d) Seconal; a barbiturate. See BARBITURATE; SECONAL.

red dirt marijuana *n.* (d) Marijuana that is growing wild and uncultivated. See MARIJUANA.

red jacket *n.* (d) Seconal. See SECONAL.

redneck *n.* (d) **1.** White person. **2.** Southern white bigot.

red oil *n.* (d) Extracted marijuana.

red wings *n.* (m) Worn on a jacket to signify having had oral intercourse with a female during her menstrual period.

reefer *n.* (d) Marijuana cigarette. See MARIJUANA CIGARETTE.

re-enter *v.* (d) Return from a drug trip; come down from the effects of a drug. **a.k.a.** come down.

re-entry *n.* (d) The return from a drug trip; the loss of drug-induced sensations.

register *v.* **1.** (d) Draw blood into an eyedropper or syringe to make sure the needle is in a vein. **2.** Understand—eg. *Does that register?*

rep *n.* **1.** Reputation. **2.** How one is rated in a group; one's status in a group.

Resistors *n.* Organization that believes in resisting induction into the military service due to religious or moral beliefs. Some men choose jail and some go to live in Canada. See C.O.

R.G. *n.* (h) Real girl (since homosexuals refer to themselves as girls).

ride *v.* **1.** Pester; annoy; aggravate—eg. *Don't ride me.* **2.** Have sexual intercourse with. See COPULATE.

riff *n.* **1.** Extra topic brought into a conversation that has no particular meaning in the conversation. **2.** Argument. **3.** (mu) From jazz slang, where it means a solo break.

right Expression used in a sentence; rhetorical question of the listener's awareness—eg. *We went to see this car, right. Then we went and talked to the man, right . . ."* See DIG.

right on Expression meaning groovy; you hit it right on the head; perfect; keep doing it. See GROOVY.

righteous *adj.* **1.** (d) Good quality (drug). **2.** Particularly good at a specific thing—eg. *You are a righteous doctor.* **3.** Honest; trustworthy; just; upright; doing what is right. **4.** Self-righteous.

rim *v.* Orally copulate the anus. **a.k.a.** ream.

rim job *n.* Oral copulation of the anus. See DINGLE BERRY; REAM JOB.

rip off *v.* **1.** Steal. **2.** Have sexual intercourse—eg. *Let's rip one off.* See COPULATE. **3.** Kill—eg. *Rip him off.* **a.k.a.** snuff, take off, zap, zonk.

ripped *adj.* **1.** (d) Very high on drugs. See LOADED. **2.** Drunk. See LOADED. **3.** Unable to function.

Ritalin *n.* (med) (methylphenidate hydrochloride; CIBA Laboratory) Mild stimulant and anti-depressant used as a mood elevator.

roach *n.* (d) End portion of a marijuana cigarette too small to hold with the fingers. When the butt is too small to smoke, the marijuana is taken out and put back into the supply, swallowed, or put in a pipe or regular cigarette. **a.k.a.** Seed. See COCKTAIL; ROACH CLIP.

roach clip *n.* Holder for the end of a marijuana cigarette too small to hold with the fingers. It can be made from a paper match, a paper clip or just about anything. Decorative ones can be purchased. **a.k.a.** clip, crutch, jefferson airplane, roach holder, roach pick. See ROACH.

roach position *n.* (d) Way of holding a marijuana cigarette with the first and second fingers and the thumb, the lighted end being shielded by the palm of the hand forming a half-moon position that prevents the smoke from escaping.

road, on the See ON THE ROAD.

rod *n.* Penis. See PENIS.

rod, on the See ON THE ROD.

rojita (*Spanish* rō-hē′-tah) *n.* Red; Seconal. See BARBITURATE; SECONAL.

roll (d) *v.* Make a marijuana cigarette. **a.k.a.** roll up. *n.* Aluminum foil containing ten pills.

roll up *v.* (d) Make a marijuana cigarette. **a.k.a.** roll.

roll your own *v.* Make your own tobacco or marijuana cigarettes.

roller *n.* (d) Vein that is difficult to inject because it moves around from the pressure exerted by the insertion of the needle.

rolling buzz *n.* (d) Initial feeling of being high after smoking marijuana or taking any drug. See RUSH.

rolling machine *n.* (d) Device used to roll either marijuana or tobacco into cigarette form.

root *n.* (d) **1.** Amphetamine; an upper. **a.k.a.** cartwheel, heart. See AMPHETAMINE. **2.** Marijuana cigarette. See MARIJUANA CIGARETTE.

rough stuff *n.* (d) Marijuana as it comes from the plant—raw, unrefined. See MARIJUANA.

rough trade *n.* (h) Vicious or dangerous homosexual.

round and round *adv.* Describes talk without meaning or coherence, continuously—eg. *He went round and round.*

round eye *n.* (p) Anus. **a.k.a.** ass hole. See GET SOME ROUND EYE.

rowdy *n.* **1.** (d) Glue sniffer. Glue sniffing is a teen-age habit, a preliminary to an increased use of drugs. It usually causes brain damage quicker than inhalation of anything else. **2.** Loud-mouth; one who often engages in physical fights.

rubber *n.* Prophylactic. **a.k.a.** skin.

rubbery *adj.* Wishy-washy; unable to make up one's mind.

ruca (*Spanish* rōō'-kah) *n.* Girl. See FEMALE.

rumble *n.* **1.** Police in a neighborhood who are there for the purpose of a shakedown or search. See SHAKEDOWN. **2.** Gang fight.

rummy *n.* Intoxicated person; a drunk—eg. *He looks like a rummy.*

rump *v.* (B) Be on heroin—eg. *He's rumping.*

run *v.* (d) **1.** Take a drug continually for an extended period of time. **2.** Go to Mexico to purchase marijuana. *n.* **1.** (m) Extended ride on a motorcycle—eg. *They made a run to get stolen goods to the fence.* **2.** (d) Amphetamine high. **3.** (d) Period of addiction—eg. *John had a two-year run of heroin.*

run, make a See MAKE A RUN.

run, on the See ON THE RUN.

run a make *v.* (p) Conduct a police check on a person to see if there is a warrant out for his arrest, done by radio.

run it *v.* Get stolen goods to a fence. See FENCE.

runner *n.* Person carrying a drug between buyer and seller.

rush *n.* First feeling one gets directly after injecting a drug, usually accompanied by the sensation of being able to taste the drug. Janis Joplin, in her last interview said, "Life is a rush." **a.k.a.** flash, jolt, rolling buzz, zing.

S

S & M *n.* **1.** A sado-masochist. **2.** A slave master, the controlling person in a sado-masochistic relationship.

sacred mushroom *n.* (d) A mushroom that is known for its hallucinogenic properties. Psilocybin, the hallucinogenic alkaloid found in these mushrooms, can also be synthesized. **a.k.a.** magic mushroom, teonanacatl. See HALLUCINOGEN; PSILOCYBIN.

salt *n.* (d) Powdered heroin. This term is used mainly in the U.S. See HEROIN.

salt shot *n.* (d) Injection of a solution of salt and water used to counteract an opiate or barbiturate overdose.

salty *adj.* Arrogant; sardonic.

sam *n.* (d) Federal narcotics agent. **a.k.a.** fuzz, narc, narco, wisher. See FED.

satch cotton *n.* (d) Cotton used to strain drugs before injection. It may be used again, if one's supply of a drug is gone, by extracting the residue of the drug. **a.k.a.** cotton. See POUND COTTON.

saying something *adj.* (B) Non-verbal communication; extremely attractive—eg. *She's really saying something.*

scabbed *adj.* **1.** Cheated. **2.** (d) Given bag drugs; cheated on a drug purchase.

scag *n.* **1.** (d) Heroin. See HEROIN. **2.** Ugly female. See FEMALE.

scam *n.* **1.** (B) Occurrence of interest—eg. *What's the scam?* = *What's happening?* **a.k.a.** hap. **2.** Story; line; lie. **a.k.a.** flam, front, put on. **3.** Con game. See CON GAME.

scarf *v.* **1.** Eat. **a.k.a.** chow down, tank up. **2.** Be a hog, unsharing, selfish. **3.** Have oral copulation. **a.k.a.** eat out. See ORAL COPULATION.

scarf a joint *v.* (d) Swallow a marijuana cigarette, usually done to avoid detection. Joint is a marijuana cigarette.

scar *n.* (d) Mark left on the arm from use of needles. See TRACK.

scat *n.* (d) Heroin. See HEROIN.

scene *n.* **1.** Place of action. See MAKE THE SCENE. **2.** Experience. **3.** Relationship—eg. *What's your scene with her?*

scheme on *v.* **1.** Flirt with. **2.** Hustle another for sexual satisfaction or the end result.

schlong *n.* Penis. Originally from Yiddish. See PENIS.

schmack *n.* (d) Heroin. From the Yiddish word *schmeck*, which means to sniff. See HEROIN.

schmeck *n.* (d) Heroin. From the Yiddish word *schmeck*, which means to sniff. See HEROIN.

schmecker *n.* (d) Heroin addict. Comes from schmeck. See SCHMECK.

schmekel (shme′-kəl) *n.* **1.** Yiddish word for a small schmuck, which means penis. See SCHMUCK. **2.** Derogatory term meaning stupid person. **a.k.a.** schmuck.

schmuck (shmuk) *n.* **1.** Yiddish word meaning penis. See PENIS. **2.** Derogatory term meaning bastard, idiot, dumb person. **a.k.a.** schmekel.

school boy *n.* (d) **1.** User of cocaine. **2.** Codeine. **a.k.a.** cubes. See CODEINE.

scoff *v.* Eat. *n.* Food.

scope out *v.* **1.** See what's happening to someone, something or at some place. **a.k.a.** check out. **2.** Learn about; look into. **a.k.a.** check out.

score *v.* **1.** (d) Obtain any form of drug. **a.k.a.** cop, make a strike. **2.** Pick up a person; establish a relationship; have sexual relations with someone. See COPULATE.

scrambler *n.* (m) Motorcycle used for mountain or hill riding. **a.k.a.** dirt bike.

scratch *v.* **1.** Forget; delete; omit something that has gone wrong. **2.** (d) Search for drugs. *n.* Money. See MONEY.

screaming *adj.* Word that intensifies a noun. **a.k.a.** flaming.

screw *v.* **1.** Have sexual intercourse. See COPULATE. **2.** Take advantage; undermine; do out of—eg. *We'll screw him out of his share.*

screw over See FUCK OVER.

screw up *v.* Make mistakes; mess things up.

screwed *adj.* Taken advantage of; undermined; done out of—eg. *He got screwed.*

screwed up *adj.* Neurotic; incapable; mixed up.

script *n.* Medical prescription. **a.k.a.** per, reader.

scuffer *n.* (B) Prostitute. See PROSTITUTE.

scuffle *v.* (B) Pick someone up for purpose of sex.

scuz *n.* Dirty, ugly, disgusting person.

scuzzy *adj.* Describes someone who is dirty, ugly, disgusting.

S.D.S. *n.* Students for a Democratic Society.

sea *n.* Cocaine. From the song "Puff (The Magic Dragon)." See COCAINE.

seafood *n.* (h) Homosexual sailor

seccy *n.* Seconal; a barbiturate. See BARBITURATE; SECONAL.

Seconal (sek'-a-nəl) *n.* (secobarbital; Eli Lilly and Company) Short-acting sedative and hypnotic having a very prompt onset of effect. **a.k.a.** border, Canadian bouncer, colorado, doll, lilly, Mexican jumping bean, pink, P.D., R.D., red, red bird, red devil, red jacket, rojito, seccy, seggy, stumbler.

sedative *n.* (med) Medication that calms excitement and activity.

seed (d) Butt of a marijuana cigarette. **a.k.a.** roach. See COCKTAIL; ROACH CLIP.

seggy *n.* Seconal; a barbiturate. See BARBITURATE; SECONAL.

self-injection position If an individual does not have anything to cut off the circulation in his arm (necessary to inject a drug), he sits on the floor with his legs crossed, puts his arm through his legs, using his legs to cut the circulation of blood in his arm, and injects the drug with his free hand. See PUMP UP; TIE OFF; TIE UP.

serum hepatitis *n.* (med) Acute infection of the liver. It can be fatal. The symptoms are headaches, stomach pains, bile in the urine, and jaundice. It is common among drug addicts who take drugs by injection. It is often contracted through lack of sterilization of the needle, the syringe or the injected material itself.

serve time *v.* (p) Serve a prison sentence. **a.k.a.** do bird, do time.

session *n.* **1.** (d) Duration of time spent in a state of being high on a drug, usually refers to LSD. **2.** (mu) Gathering of musicians for purpose of playing music. **3.** Sexual activity.

set 1. (d) Two Seconals and one amphetamine. **2.** (mu) Jam session. **3.** (mu) All the songs musicians play in one 45-minute period. **4.** Gathering of people; a party. **5.** Discussion. **6.** Person's group of friends—eg. *Joe's set is here.* **7.** Mental state. Comes from the psychological term.

set up *v.* (d) **1.** Catch a drug user by having an informer sell him drugs in front of a narcotics officer. **2.** Hide drugs in a user's house, then raid it to arrest him. **a.k.a.** plant. *n.* Act of setting someone up for arrest; plant.

setting *n.* **1.** Surrounding. **2.** (d) Where a person uses a drug. Usually more important when taking LSD than any other drugs.

settle *v.* Accept; be non-selective—eg. *I'll settle for what you have.*

sexual variations See BEADS; MAZOLA PARTY; VIBRATOR; WESSON PARTY; WHIPPED CREAM.

shack up (with) *v.* **1.** Live with someone without being married. **2.** Have sexual intercourse with. See COPULATE.

shades *n.* Sunglasses. Usually worn by people using drugs to protect their eyes, which are often light-sensitive and either dilated or constricted by the light. Also worn to avoid detection as a drug user. At present, sunglasses of various colors are worn also at night indoors as a part of fashion. **a.k.a.** specs.

shaft *v.* **1.** Take advantage of. **2.** Drop; fire: throw out.

shafted *adj.* **1.** Taken advantage of. **2.** Dropped; fired; thrown out.

shakedown *v.* Search; look for something. *n.* (p) Attempt at extortion.

sheen *n.* (B) Car. See CAR.

shelf, on the See ON THE SHELF.

shine *v.* Ignore; consciously disregard; not pay attention; not listen. Used in expressions *Shine, baby, shine* and *Shine it on.* **a.k.a.** drive over something.

shine on See SHINE.

shit *n.* **1.** (d) Heroin. **a.k.a.** ca-ca. See HEROIN. **2.** (d) Marijuana. **a.k.a.** ca-ca. See MARIJUANA. **3.** Fecal matter. **a.k.a.** crap, dong. **4.** Exclamation of disgust—eg. *Oh, shit!*

shit can *v.* **1.** Throw away; discard. **2.** Do wrong to a person one feels deserves it—eg. *I'm going to shit can him.* *n.* Toilet.

shit head *n.* **1.** Unreliable person. **a.k.a.** fuck head, fuck off. **2.** Nasty, mean person. **a.k.a.** low life. **3.** (d) Drug user, mainly heroin but also marijuana.

shmeck *n.* (d) Heroin. Comes from the Yiddish term *schmeck*, meaning to sniff. It is used mainly in the U.S. See HEROIN.

shmee *n.* (d) Heroin. Term is used mainly in the U.S. See HEROIN.

shoe polish *n.* Substance sniffed to obtain a high.

shook up *adj.* Worried; nervous.

shoot *v.* Inject a drug. **a.k.a.** shoot up.

shoot down *v.* **1.** Criticize negatively. **2.** Reject—eg. *You can shoot him down with one look.*

shoot gravy *v.* (d) Reinject a solution of blood and drugs that has clogged in the syringe and been heated to make it liquid again. Gravy refers to the mixed solution.

shoot marbles *v.* Play, shoot, throw dice.

shoot up *v.* Inject a drug. **a.k.a.** shoot.
shooting gallery *n.* Place to go to shoot drugs, eg., someone's house. **a.k.a.** acid pad, launching pad. See PAD.
short *v.* Cheat. *n.* Car. See CAR.
short arm *n.* Penis. See PENIS.
short but *n.* (d) Drug purchase in small quantities.
short con *n.* Small-time confidence game. See CON GAME.
short count *n.* (d) Lesser amount than what was said to be when selling drugs.
shot *n.* **1.** (d) An injection of a narcotic. See INJECTION. **2.** Critical remark—eg. *You didn't have to make that shot. adj.* Non-functional—eg. *He's shot.*
shotgun *v.* (d) Put the lighted end of a marijuana cigarette in your mouth and blow smoke through it into another person's mouth.
shotgun, sit See SIT SHOTGUN.
shrink *n.* Psychologist or psychiatrist. Comes from head shrinker. **a.k.a.** head shrinker, psych.
shrink someone's head *v.* Figure someone out; discuss a person's problems almost to the exclusion of other topics of conversation.
shtup (shtoop) *v.* Have sexual intercourse—eg. *Does she shtup?* See COPULATE.
shuck *v.* **1.** Bullshit. See BULLSHIT. **2.** Con. See CON. **3.** (B) Kid; joke. **a.k.a.** shuckin. *n.* **1.** Bullshit. See BULLSHIT. **2.** Con. See CON.
shut down *v.* **1.** Condemn; criticize; reject. **2.** Stop someone or something.
sick *adj.* (d) Having withdrawal symptoms. See WITHDRAWAL.
sickie *n.* Person who is mentally ill.
signify *v.* Boast; show off; show good things about oneself but not in a direct way, eg., drive around a building a couple of times in your expensive car
silk *n.* (B) White person.
simon (*Spanish* sē-mōn') Yes.
singularly *adj.* Solely; totally; without a doubt.

sissy *n.* **1.** (h) Male homosexual. See HOMOSEXUAL. **2.** Mama's boy. **3.** Coward.

sister *n.* (B) Black female. See BROTHER.

sit shotgun *v.* Sit on the passenger side in the front seat of a car. Comes from old cowboy movies: riding shotgun on a stagecoach.

sitter *n.* (d) Experienced hallucinogen user who helps to guide a new user through a drug experience. **a.k.a.** guide, guru, tour guide.

sixteenth *n.* (d) One-sixteenth of an ounce of a drug, usually heroin. See QUANTITIES OF DRUGS.

skin *n.* **1.** (B) Handshake; an initial greeting upon meeting. The expression is *Gimme some skin.* **2.** (d) Intramuscular injection. **a.k.a.** job off, pop, skin pop. **3.** (d) Cigarette paper, used to roll one's own. **4.** Prophylactic. **a.k.a.** rubber.

skin pop (d) Inject a drug under the skin, not into a vein; inject intramuscularly or subcutaneously. The onset of the drug is not as fast as with intravenous injection. **a.k.a.** pop. See MAINLINE. *n.* Intramuscular injection. **a.k.a.** job off, pop, skin.

skinny *n.* Truth—eg. *I want the skinny.*

skipper *v.* Travel about with all one's belongings; sleep rough; bed down with others in others' homes. See CRASH PAD; ON THE ROAD; SLEEP ROUGH.

skull job *n.* Oral copulation of the vagina. See CUNNILINGUS; ORAL COPULATION.

sky piece *n.* (B) Hat. **a.k.a.** lid.

slams *n.* (p) Jail; prison—eg. *The bims went bam and threw me in the slams.* See CLINK.

slave *n.* **1.** Woman. **2.** Job. **a.k.a.** gig.

sleep rough *v.* Sleep anywhere. See CRASH PAD; ON THE ROAD; SKIPPER.

sleeper *n.* (d) Barbiturate; sleeping pill. See BARBITURATE.

sleigh ride *v* Take cocaine—eg. *I'm going to sleigh ride.* *n.* Effects of having taken cocaine—eg. *He's on a sleigh ride.*

slide *v.* Leave; depart. See LEAVE.

slide, let something See LET SOMETHING SLIDE.

slit *n.* Vagina. See VAGINA.

slogans Many standard, acceptable slogans that are used for purposes of advertising are being given underground meanings and used on signs and posters. See BE AWARE; KEEP OFF THE GRASS; SPEED KILLS; SUPPORT YOUR LOCAL TRAVEL AGENT.

slut *n.* Whore. See PROSTITUTE.

smack *n.* Heroin. See HEROIN.

smackse (smak'-zē) (d) Needle used for injecting drugs.

small time *adj.* **1.** (d) Using the less addictive drugs. **2.** Lacking in status—eg. *He's a small-time hustler.*

smashed *adj.* Very high on drugs or alcohol. See LOADED.

smoke *v.* (d) Implies smoking a marijuana cigarette —eg. *Let's smoke.* *n.* Wood alcohol.

smokey *adj.* Good; groovy. See GROOVY.

smudge *n.* (d) Small amount of heroin. See QUANTITIES OF DRUGS.

snag *v.* Catch; apprehend. *n.* Something that goes wrong.

snagged *adj.* **1.** Caught. **2.** Delayed or otherwise inconvenienced by something going wrong.

snap *v.* **1.** Go through mental changes. Can be while on a drug or after taking a drug. See CHANGES; GO THROUGH CHANGES. **2.** Change thoughts rapidly. **3.** Lose grasp on reality. **a.k.a.** flip, flip out.

snapper *n.* **1.** (d) Amyl nitrite. See AMYL NITRITE. **2.** Vagina. Comes from contraction of vaginal muscles during intercourse—eg. *I want some snapper = I would like to have sexual intercourse. Let's fuck!* See VAGINA.

snatch *n.* **1.** Vagina. See VAGINA. **2.** Female. See FEMALE.

snatch someone up *v.* Beat up; beat the shit out of.

sneeze it out *v.* (d) Attempt to break the drug habit.

sniff *v.* **1.** (d) Inhale through the nostrils. Dopers sniff breath fresheners, gasoline, glue, lacquer, paint, shoe polish, etc. **a.k.a.** blow the bag, horn, snort. **2.** Put out; stop. **a.k.a.** sniff out.

sniff glue *v.* (d) Inhale model-airplane glue. The resultant effects include double vision, feeling of euphoria, and hallucinations. This practice causes organic brain damage. See GLUE SNIFF.

snort *v.* Sniff or inhale a drug through the nostrils. **a.k.a.** blow the bag, horn, sniff.

snow *v.* **1.** Fool; put something over on—eg. *I snowed him.* **2.** Overwhelm; be too much to handle. *n.* (d) **1.** Cocaine. Comes from the white color and crystals of the drug. See COCAINE. **2.** Heroin. Comes from its white color. See HEROIN.

snow job *v.* Cheat; do out of. **a.k.a.** con. *n.* Persuasive but insincere talk or writing—eg. *He pulled a real snow job on him.*

snowbird *n.* User of cocaine. Comes from snow, which means cocaine.

snuff *v.* **1.** Eliminate; stop; put an end to someone's activities. **2.** Knock someone out. **3.** Kill someone. **a.k.a.** rip off, take off, zap, zonk.

S.O.B. *n.* Son of a bitch.

sock it to me! **1.** Can be sexual, "it" referring to sexual intercourse. **a.k.a.** whip it to me! **2.** Give it to me. **3.** Keep it up; you're doing well.

sodium amytal (sō'-dē-əm am'-i-tal) *n.* (med) Moderately rapid-acting sedative and hypnotic.

sodium pentothal (sō'-dē-əm pen'-tah-thɔl) *n.* (med) Used as an anesthetic agent for brief surgical procedures and for control of convulsions. **a.k.a.** truth serum.

soft drug *n.* Hallucinogenic drug that is not physically addictive. The opposite of hard drug, such as heroin or morphine. **a.k.a.** light stuff. See HARD DRUG.

soles *n.* (B) Shoes **a.k.a.** stumps.

solid *n.* (d) Cigarette made from marijuana and tobacco. *adj.* Very agreeable to one's attitudes—eg. *That's solid, man.*

soma *n.* (d) Fly-agaric, "the divine mushroom of immortality." A bright-red mushroom, indigenous to birch-forests, and known for its hallucinogenic properties. Soma is one of the most ancient religious inebriates, and its name comes from that of the Hindu god, Soma. **a.k.a.** magic mushroom. See HALLUCINOGEN.

soul *n.* An inherent quality Black people feel they have and whites rarely do. It implies an awareness and understanding of life, a naturalness of expression, being in contact with the naturalness of life and the environment, understanding yourself and others. The term is often used for one connected with the arts in a meaningful manner. See SOUL BROTHER; SOUL FOOD; SOUL MUSIC; SOUL ROLL; SOUL SISTER.

soul brother *n.* (B) Black person. Term used by Blacks primarily. See SOUL SISTER.

soul food *n.* Black-style food, originally from the South: chitlings, black-eyed peas, greens, ham hocks, B.B.Q. ribs, corn bread, etc.

soul music *n.* Black-style rock-and-roll music; the Motown sound (Motown is a Black-owned record company). The music is characterized by a strong beat.

soul roll *n.* (B) Sexual intercourse between people who are emotionally involved with each other. Concept comes from the idea that you are rolling with another's soul, not just his body; implying a deep emotional (not necessarily long-lasting) involvement. See HEAD THING.

soul sister *n.* Black female. Term used by Blacks primarily. See SOUL BROTHER.

sound *v.* (d) Ask, question.

sounds *n.* (B) Music.

source *n.* (d) Supplier of drugs. See PUSHER.

South African hash *n.* (d) A form of hashish. See HASHISH.

spaced *adj.* (d) **1.** High, not necessarily from drugs Term may come from the feeling of floating from hallucinogenic drugs. **2.** Out of contact with real-

spaced out

ity. The less contact you have with reality the more spaced you are. See SPACED OUT.

spaced out *adj.* **1.** (d) High on a drug. See LOADED. **2.** Out of touch with reality, not necessarily on a drug. See SPACED.

spade *n.* (B) Black person.

Spanish fly *n.* An aphrodisiac. Originally used with animals to create a desire to mate; currently used with humans to create a desire for sexual intercourse.

spansula *n.* Combination of amphetamines and barbiturates. **a.k.a.** G.B., goofball, speedball. See AMPHETAMINE; BARBITURATE.

sparkle plenty *n.* Amphetamine; an upper. See AMPHETAMINE.

S.P.C.H. *n.* Society for Prevention of Cruelty to Homosexuals.

specs *n.* **1.** Sunglasses. **a.k.a.** shades. **2.** Eyeglasses.

speed *v.* (d) **1.** Take Methedrine. **2.** Feel the effects of Methedrine—eg. *He's speeding.* *n.* (d) Amphetamine; an upper. Usually refers to Methedrine. See AMPHETAMINE; METHEDRINE.

speed freak *n.* Individual who compulsively uses amphetamines and/or Methedrine. See AMPHETAMINE; FREAK; METHEDRINE.

Speed kills Slogan meaning Methedrine is dangerous. Speed is Methedrine. The original slogan is from safe-driving campaigns.

speedball *n.* Injection of a mixture of stimulant and depressant, usually heroin and cocaine or Methedrine and a barbiturate. **a.k.a.** G.B., goofball, spansula. See BLACK AND WHITE, BLACK AND WHITE MINSTREL, BLACK BOMBER, DOMINO, FRENCH BLUE, MINSTREL, PURPLE HEART.

speeder *n.* One who has had too much amphetamine and is constantly moving or jerking. See AMPHETAMINE.

spent *adj.* **1.** Overwhelmed; incapable of further activity. **2.** Worn out; exhausted. **3.** Already climaxed (sexually).

spiffie See SPIFFY.

spiffy *adj.* Groovy; fantastic. The term is very old and is now used sarcastically when a person thinks he looks good and another person doesn't think so. See GROOVY.

spike *n.* (d) Needle or syringe used for injection. Unsterilized needles can cause hepatitis. See FIT; SERUM HEPATITIS.

spiked *adj.* **1.** High on drugs. See LOADED. **2.** Describes punch with alcohol added.

splib (splib) *n.* Derogatory term for a Black male.

spliff *n.* (d) Marijuana cigarette. See MARIJUANA CIGARETTE.

split *v.* Go; leave; depart. See LEAVE.

split beaver *n.* **1.** A look at a woman's vagina (or underpants) because of the way she is sitting. **a.k.a.** beaver shot, spread beaver. **2.** A photograph of a woman with her legs spread, showing the vagina and pubic area. **a.k.a.** beaver shot, spread beaver.

splurge *v.* Leave; depart. See LEAVE.

spook *n.* Black person. Can be derogatory when used by whites.

spooky *adj.* Unusual; weird; strange. Usually associated with the occult, referring to circumstances that are unexplainable under normal conditions.

spoon *v.* Method of using the tongue to enter the vagina and caress the clitoris during cunnilingus. See CUNNILINGUS; ORAL COPULATION. *n.* (d) **1.** Bent spoon used for preparing and heating a crystallized drug for injection. See COOK. **2.** Two grams of heroin. See QUANTITIES OF DRUGS.

spoonful *n.* (d) Tablespoon of powdered or crystalline drug; approximately two grams of a drug.

spot you *v.* (d) Pay first and take delivery of a drug later.

spread *v.* Share. *adj.* Describes a position with the legs apart showing the vaginal area. See SPLIT BEAVER; SPREAD BEAVER.

spread beaver *n.* **1.** A look at a woman's vagina (or underpants) because of the way she is sitting.

a.k.a. beaver shot, split beaver. **2.** A photograph of a woman with her legs spread, showing the vagina and pubic area. **a.k.a.** beaver shot, split beaver.

square *n.* Tobacco cigarette. **a.k.a.** dirt, hole, square joint, straight. *adj.* **1.** (d) Describes a person who doesn't use drugs. **2.** Refers to a person with a conventional and provincial attitude. **a.k.a.** lame, straight. **3.** (d) Describes a non-addict. Usage comes from Synanon. See SYNANON FOUNDATION.

square joint *n.* Tobacco cigarette. **a.k.a.** dirt, hole, square, straight. See JOINT; SQUARE.

squatter *n.* Individual who moves from commune to commune in the hippy community, living at each one for a short period of time. See COMMUNE; SKIPPER.

squirrelly *adj.* Stupid; foolish.

S.S. *n.* (p) Suspended sentence.

stack *n.* (d) Quantity of marijuana cigarettes.

stag *adj.* Composed of or presented for men only. *adv.* Without a date. See DRAG.

stag movie *n.* Erotic 8-mm. film usually of people engaging in oral and sexual intercourse and also of humans and animals in sexual play.

stallion *n.* (B) Large woman, attractive, sexy. **a.k.a.** amazon. See FEMALE.

star dust *n.* (d) Cocaine. See COCAINE.

stash *n.* (d) **1.** Individual's personal supply of drugs. **2.** Place where drugs and drug paraphernalia are hidden. **a.k.a.** trap.

stay *v.* Keep an erection.

steamboat *n.* (d) Pipe for smoking marijuana. See HOOKAH.

step *v.* Do things; initiate activities—eg. *Let's get steppin'*.

Stepin Fetchit *n.* Name of a Black actor of the 30s and 40s. His character was of bulging eyes, tap dancing, smiling, saying "Yessuh, boss, I'se comin'" and shuffling. His name can refer to an Uncle Tom. See UNCLE TOM.

stew *n.* **1.** Airline hostess; stewardess. **2.** Synanon marathon; long group-therapy session. See SYNANON FOUNDATION.

stick *n.* Marijuana cigarette. See MARIJUANA CIGARETTE.

stiff *v.* Cheat; rob, **a.k.a.** sting. *n.* Dead body.

stiffed *adj.* Drunk. See LOADED.

sting *v.* Steal; cheat; rob—eg. *I was stung for $50.00.* **a.k.a.** stiff.

stir, in See IN STIR.

stomp *v.* Beat up physically or verbally. *n.* Activity common in junior and senior high schools. Someone throws a coin on the ground and a number of people try to cover it with one foot or pick it up. Called nickel stomp, penny stomp.

stompin' ground *n.* **1.** (B) Home. See HOME. **2.** Territory; neighborhood.

stone *adv.* Very—eg. *stone fox, stone soul, stone drunk.*

stone addict *n.* (d) One who has a heavy habit. See STONE.

stoned *adj.* **1.** (d) Experiencing the feelings of or being under the effects of a drug; high. See LOADED. **2.** Drunk. See LOADED.

stoner *n.* (d) Person who takes and gets high on drugs frequently. See STONED.

stony *adj.* (d) Pertaining to frequent and excessive use of drugs; displaying characteristics of a drug user—eg. *He is a stony guy.*

stool *v.* Give or sell information to the police; inform. See STOOL PIGEON; STOOLIE.

stool pigeon *n.* (p) Informer; one who gives or sells information to the police. **a.k.a.** stoolie.

stoolie *n.* (p) Informer. **a.k.a.** stool pigeon.

story *n.* **1.** Occurrences. **2.** Lie; alibi. **3.** Life style. **a.k.a.** bag, bit.

S.T.P. (DOM: 2,5 dimethoxy-4-methylphene-thylamine; Dow Chemical Co.) Synthetic hallucinogen similar to LSD. It is very potent and long-acting; its effects last longer than those of LSD. STP stands for Serenity, Tranquillity, Peace. The initials are also associated with a car motor-oil additive of the same name, and the decals advertising it are used to symbolize the drug. See DOM; HALLUCINOGEN.

straight *n.* Ordinary tobacco cigarette (without marijuana). a.k.a. dirt, hole, square, square joint. *adj.* **1.** (d) Off drugs; clean. **2.** A drug addict will use the word "straight" to mean to use a drug—eg. *I've got to get straight.* **3.** Not homosexual. **4.** (mu) Everything's O.K. Jazz musicians use it this way. **5.** Clear-cut; without lying or rationalizing. **6.** Establishment-oriented. a.k.a. lame, square. See ESTABLISHMENT. **7.** Legal; within the law. See GO STRAIGHT.

straight shooter *n.* Honest, virtuous person. See STRAIGHT.

strange *adj.* **1.** Peculiar; odd; extremely out of the ordinary, almost mystic. **2.** Not comprehendible.

strap *v.* Have sexual intercourse. See COPULATE.

strap on *v.* Have sexual intercourse. See COPULATE.

street, on the See ON THE STREET.

strike *n.* (d) Dose of a drug. a.k.a. hit.

strip *v.* Shave

strobe *v.* (d) Have the visual effect described below while under the influence of certain drugs. *n.* Light that affects visual perception by an extremely rapid flashing. One sees movement in a non-continuous way, a stopping-and-starting effect.

stroke *v.* **1.** Have sexual intercourse. See COPULATE. **2.** Praise. *n.* Compliment—eg. *Give me some strokes.*

stroke the lizard *v.* Masturbate. See MASTURBATE.

strung out *adj.* (d) **1.** So addicted to drugs that one cannot physically do without them. **2.** On a drug.

stud *n.* **1.** Male. **2.** One whose masculinity is beyond question due to the fact that it is proved at every possible moment, usually through sexual encounters.

stuff *n.* (d) **1.** Heroin. Stuff principally refers to heroin. See HEROIN. **2.** Any kind of drug.

stum *n.* (d) **1.** Marijuana. See MARIJUANA. **2.** Sleeping pill. Comes from stumbler. See BARBITURATE; STUMBLER.

stumbler *n.* Seconal; a barbiturate. See BARBITURATE; SECONAL.

stumbles, have the See HAVE THE STUMBLES.

stumps *n.* (d) Shoes. **a.k.a.** soles.

stung *adj.* **1.** Apprehended; caught. Especially in buying drugs. **2.** Cheated or robbed.

sucker *n.* Person who can be used or taken advantage of easily. **a.k.a.** easy mark, fish mark. See CON.

suede *n.* **1.** Black person. **2.** (d) Liquid solution of opium-pipe residue. **a.k.a.** suey. *adj.* Black suey.

suey *n.* (d) Liquid solution of opium-pipe residue. **a.k.a.** suede.

sugar *n.* **1.** (B) Kiss; kisses—eg. *Give me some sugar*. **2.** (d) LSD. See HALLUCINOGEN; LYSERGIC ACID DIETHYLAMIDE. **3.** (d) Powdered narcotic.

sugar down *v.* Add sugar or another substance to heroin or any white powdered drug to increase the amount of powder to obtain a larger quantity. Done to cheat the buyer. **a.k.a.** CUT.

sugar lump *n.* (d) LSD. See HALLUCINOGEN; LYSERGIC ACID DIETHYLAMIDE.

sunshine *n.* (d) Orange or yellow tablet of LSD. **a.k.a.** orange, yellow.

super *adj.* **1.** Intensifies any word it comes before—eg. *a super miniskirt*. **2.** An exclamation meaning great; fantastic. See GROOVY.

super pot *n.* A way to get high. Surgical spirit (95% alcohol) is boiled and then injected into a regular cigarette and smoked.

supplies *n.* (d) Drugs and all accessories needed to take or inject the drugs. See COOK; FIT.

Support your local travel agent Slogan meaning support your seller of drugs (especially LSD) or the person who is with you on your LSD trip (guide). From the slogan: Support your local police.

sweet, no See NO SWEAT.

sweet *n.* (d) Amphetamine; an upper. See AMPHETAMINE. *adj.* Homosexual. **a.k.a.** fay, gay. See HOMOSEXUAL.

sweet lucy *n.* (d) Marijuana. See MARIJUANA.

sweet meat *n.* (B) Female. See FEMALE.

swing *v.* Go to swing parties. See SWING PARTY; SWINGER.

swing on *v.* Fight with; beat up; attack.

swing party *n.* Party where people engage in sexual play and intercourse, changing partners or in groups of three or more. **a.k.a.** orgy.

swinger *n.* **1.** Person who is socially knowledgeable. **2.** (d) One who uses all forms of drugs. **3.** Person who engages in varied sexual activities, eg., orgies, groups. See SWING; SWING PARTY.

swingman *n.* (d) **1.** Dealer of drugs. **2.** Connection. See CONNECTION.

swish *v.* (h) Walk in an effeminate manner, making hip movements. Used when describing a male homosexual's walk.

swish in *v.* (h) Enter walking like an effeminate homosexual—eg. *He swished in.*

switch hitter *n.* One who is bisexual. See AC-DC; BI.

swoop *v.* Refers to being surrounded or engulfed, usually by police, who are said to swoop down on drug users.

Synanon Foundation *n.* Non-profit foundation that initially specialized in drug rehabilitation in the major cities of the U.S. Currently Synanon is using its techniques with anyone who wishes to have an emotional experience through firsthand encounter. The Synanon therapy approach is beneficial for some, detrimental for others. See GAME; SQUARE.

synthetic grass *n.* Synthetic marijuana; THC. **a.k.a.** clarabelle, clay. See TETRAHYDROCANNABINOL.

system *n.* (d) Tolerance for a drug that an addict's body has—eg. *He took too much for the system.*

t

T *n.* Marijuana. See MARIJUANA.

tab *n.* (d) **1.** Pill in tablet form. **2.** LSD capsule. **a.k.a.** pellet.

tacky *adj.* (h) Used by homosexual male to indicate the bitchiness, the complaining quality of another homosexual male who has the female role.

taco *n.* Mexican or Mexican-American. Term used by whites.

tael *n.* (d) One and one-third ounce of a drug, usually opium. See QUANTITIES OF DRUGS.

tail *n.* **1.** Sexual intercourse—eg. *I'd like to get some tail.* See COPULATION. **2.** Female. See FEMALE. **3.** (p) Parole. **4.** (p) Probation.

tail, piece of See PIECE OF TAIL.

taint *n.* The piece of skin between the penis or vagina and the anus. Called taint because "it 'taint cunt and it 'taint ass."

take a cure *v.* Stop using an addictive drug, usually in a hospital. **a.k.a.** clear up, withdraw. See CURE, THE; LEXINGTON; WINDER.

take a fall *v.* (d) Receive a jail sentence.

take off *v.* **1.** (d) Get high on a drug. See HIGH. **2.** Rob; hold up. **3.** Leave; depart. See LEAVE. **4.** (B) Kill—eg. *They took him off.* **a.k.a.** rip off, snuff, zap, zonk.

take the fall *v.* Accept the inevitable.

take the pipe *v.* **1.** Commit suicide. **2.** (d) Kill oneself via an overdose of a drug.

take your best shot Expression meaning boast. Refers to one's ability to accept all challenges; usually the shot is verbal and antagonistic, not physical.

taken off *adj.* Robbed—eg. *I got taken off by some guy last night.*

take-off artist *n.* (d) One who supports his drug habit by robbing other addicts or pushers (sellers).

talk and walk

talk and walk *v.* (p) Term applied to feigning therapeutic benefits derived in therapy sessions by saying the right things. If the right things are said, the possibility of parole is better.

talk to the canoe driver *v.* (B) Have oral copulation of the vagina. See CUNNILINGUS; ORAL COPULATION.

tall *adj.* Good.

tambourine man *n.* (d) Seller of drugs. There is a song called "Tambourine Man." See PUSHER.

tank up *v.* **1.** Eat. **a.k.a.** chow down, scarf. **2.** Drink (alcohol).

tap *v.* (d) Inject a drug by tapping the end of the syringe in order to release the drug slowly. It is similar to a sexual combination of pain and pleasure.

tar *n.* (d) Opium. See OPIUM.

Tasmanian pig *n.* Policeman in New York City, especially on the lower East Side. See POLICEMAN.

taste *n.* **1.** (B) Liquor; drink. **2.** (d) Very small amount of a drug.

T.C.B. (B) *Taking care of business.* Expression meaning do whatever needs to be done or that you plan to do.

tea *n.* (d) **1.** Marijuana. See MARIJUANA. **2.** Beverage made by brewing marijuana into a drink.

tea bag *n.* (d) Using marijuana—eg. *She's in a tea bag.* Tea is marijuana. See BAG.

tea blower *n.* (d) Marijuana smoker. Tea is marijuana.

tea head *n.* (d) User of marijuana. Tea is marijuana. See HEAD.

tecata *n.* (d) Heroin. See HEROIN.

tecate *n.* (d) User of narcotics.

teenybopper *n.* Young teen-ager; adolescent who identifies with the hippy culture. See BOPPER; FLOWER; FLOWER CHILDREN; HIPPY.

tell it like it is Be open, honest, straightforward; hold nothing back because of fear of hurting someone's feelings.

Thorazine

ten-cent bag *n.* (d) Ten-dollar quantity of a drug. **a.k.a.** dime bag, 10¢ bag. See QUANTITIES OF DRUGS.

teonanacatl *n.* (d) "God's flesh," the sacred mushroom of Middle America. Any of 14 species of small yellow mushrooms, which are hallucinogenic when eaten. Their active ingredient is psilocybin. **a.k.a.** magic mushroom, sacred mushroom. See HALLUCINOGEN; PSILOCYBIN.

terps *n.* (d) Elixir of terpin hydrate with codeine, a cough syrup.

testicles *n.* Male reproductive glands. **a.k.a.** balls, chestnuts, cojones, huevos, marshmallows, nuts.

tetrahydrocannabinol *n.* (d) THC, the active chemical compound in marijuana. It can be produced synthetically. It is taken in pill or powder form. The effects are similar to those of marijuana, but much more intense. **a.k.a.** clarabelle, clay, synthetic grass.

Texas tea *n.* (d) Marijuana. Tea is marijuana. See MARIJUANA.

THC *n.* (d) Tetrahydrocannabinol. See TETRAHYDROCANNABINOL.

there *n.* **1.** (d) When a person has reached the ultimate high on a drug experience he is considered to be *there*. See HIT THE MOON; PEAK. **2.** Place one wants to be emotionally; one's goal. See MADE IT.

thing *n.* **1.** Interest; activity. **a.k.a.** bit. See DO YOUR THING. **2.** Personal problem. **a.k.a.** bag, bit. **3.** Penis. See PENIS.

third eye *n.* Introspective insight into self that some drugs provide.

thoroughbred *n.* Person who sells only pure narcotics. Very rare. See PUSHER.

Thorazine (thɔ′-rō-zēn) *n.* (med) (chlorpromazine hydrochloride; Smith, Kline & French Laboratories). Drug used as an antidote for the ill effects of LSD. See CHLORPROMAZINE HYDROCHLORIDE.

threads

threads *n.* Clothes.

throw me out (d) Expression meaning give me some pills or supply me with drugs.

thrust *n.* (d) Amphetamine. See AMPHETAMINE.

thumb *v.* Hitchhike. **a.k.a.** hitch. *n.* Marijuana cigarette. See MARIJUANA CIGARETTE.

thumb handshake *n.* Handshake in which fingers are clasped above the wrist instead of below as in the conventional handshake.

thump *v.* Fight; beat up. **a.k.a.** get down.

thumped *adj.* Beaten up.

tick off *v.* Make angry.

ticked off *adj.* Angry.

ticket *n.* (d) LSD. Comes from the idea of a trip. See HALLUCINOGEN; LYSERGIC ACID DIETHYLAMIDE; TRIP.

tie *n.* (d) Any cord to tie around arm or leg to make vein stand up for easy injection of a drug.

tie it on *v.* **1.** (B) Give money to. **a.k.a.** lace it on. **2.** Get drunk.

tie off *v.* (d) Tie a cord around the arm to make a vein stand out for easier injection. **a.k.a.** tie up. See PUMP UP; SELF-INJECTION POSITION.

tie up *v.* (d) Tie a cord around the arm to make a vein stand out for easier injection. **a.k.a.** tie off. See PUMP UP; SELF-INJECTION POSITION.

tight *adj.* **1.** Close; intimate; good friends with—eg. *They're really tight.* **2.** Drunk. See LOADED. **3.** Stingy; selfish. **4.** Withdrawn; closed.

tight, my jaws are See MY JAWS ARE TIGHT.

tight-assed *adj.* Up tight. Used by Eldridge Cleaver in a book. See UP TIGHT.

tilde (*Spanish* tēl'-dā) *n.* Jail. See CLINK.

time, do See DO TIME.

time in motion *n.* (d) Describes the feeling that time dissolves into motion and the drug user feels motion and movement without knowledge of the passage of time.

time in space *n.* (d) Describes the feeling that time is compressed into movement and the two are synonymous; time doesn't exist (both time and motion lose their usual connotations).

tin *n.* (d) Container of marijuana, usually a pipe-tobacco tin. See PRINCE ALBERT CAN.

Tío Taco (*Spanish* tē'-ō tah'-cō) *n.* Uncle Tom. Term used by Mexican-American community. See UNCLE TOM; UNCLE TOMMYHAWK.

tit *n.* Female's breast, specifically the nipple. See BREAST.

tits *adj.* Fantastic; great; groovy—eg. *"How was the party?" "It was tits!"* See GROOVY.

T.J. *n.* Tijuana, Mexico.

T.L.C. Tender loving care.

toak *v.* (d) Puff or drag off a marijuana cigarette. **a.k.a.** toke. *n.* (d) Puff of a marijuana cigarette. **a.k.a.** toke.

together *adj.* Self-actualized; able to understand all your thoughts, ideas and ideals; knowing where you are going in life—eg. *You are really together.*

toke *v.* (d) Puff or drag off a marijuana cigarette. **a.k.a.** toak. *n.* (d) Puff of a marijuana cigarette. **a.k.a.** toak.

toke pipe *n.* (d) Pipe in which marijuana is smoked. See HOOKAH; TOKE.

toke up *v.* **1.** (d) Light up a marijuana cigarette; start smoking (not for the first time). **2.** Get ready for—eg. *I have to toke up for my exams.*

tolerance *n.* Physiological resistance the body builds up to the effects of a drug.

tom *v.* Act like an Uncle Tom. See UNCLE TOM. *n.* **1.** Uncle Tom. See UNCLE TOM. **2.** (d) An injection of a narcotic. See INJECTION.

tom mix *n.* (d) An injection of a narcotic. See INJECTION.

tombo (*Spanish* tōm'-bō) *n.* Policeman; cop. **a.k.a.** azul, chota. See POLICEMAN.

tongue *v.* **1.** (d) Inject a drug under the tongue. This avoids scars on the arms. **a.k.a.** tough. **2.** Orally copulate the vagina with extensive use of the tongue. See CUNNILINGUS, ORAL COPULATION.

too much *adj.* **1.** Overwhelming; very good—eg. *That dinner was just too much!* **2.** Exclamation of surprise or joy in response to a situation—eg. *Too much!*

tooie *n.* (d) Tuinal capsule; a barbiturate. Also spelled *tuie*. See BARBITURATE; TUINAL.

tool *n.* **1.** Someone you use to achieve your goal. **2.** Penis. See PENIS.

tools *n.* (d) Equipment used for preparing and injecting drugs. See FIT.

tootsie *n.* (d) Tuinal capsule; a barbiturate. See BARBITURATE; TUINAL.

top *n.* (d) Round top of the peyote cactus plant. **a.k.a.** button. See HALLUCINOGEN; PEYOTE.

torch up *v.* (d) Smoke marijuana.

tore up *adj.* **1.** (d) Condition resulting from use of barbiturates and amphetamines (downers and uppers) at the same time; feeling of wanting to sit down and get up simultaneously. **2.** (d) Under the influence of a drug. See LOADED. **3.** Psychologically confused. **a.k.a.** torn up.

torn up *adj.* **1.** Agitated; depressed over something or somebody—eg. *I'm torn up about her.* **2.** Psychologically confused; messed up; wasted. **a.k.a.** tore up. **3.** (d) Under the influence of a drug. See LOADED.

tosca (*Spanish* tɔs'-kah) *n.* Marijuana. See MARIJUANA.

toss out *v.* (d) Pretend to have withdrawal symptoms to induce a doctor to prescribe narcotics.

tossed *adj.* (d) Searched by the police in an attempt to find drugs.

total *v.* Completely wreck or destroy—eg. *I totaled my motorcycle.*

totaled *adj.* Completely wrecked or destroyed.

tough *v.* (d) Inject a drug under the tongue. **a.k.a.** tongue. *adj.* **1.** Attractive; good. **2.** Bad; hard to handle (situation).

tour guide *n.* (d) Experienced hallucinogen user who

helps to guide a new user through a drug experience. **a.k.a.** guide, guru, sitter.

toxy *n.* The smallest container of prepared opium See QUANTITIES OF DRUGS.

track *n.* (d) **1.** Marks made on the skin from previous injections. **a.k.a.** calling card, corn, crater, mark, scar, trail. See TRACKED UP. **2.** Vein collapsed by constant drug injection.

tracked up *adj.* (d) Scarred from needle injections. See TRACK.

trade *v.* (h) Look for action; look for someone to have sex with. See DO FOR TRADE.

trafficker (tra'-fi-kər) *n.* (d) One who sells drugs. See PUSHER.

trail *n.* (d) **1.** Visual experience; hallucination. Usually caused by use of drugs. **a.k.a.** cartoon, pattern. **2.** Scar made by needle from injecting a drug. See TRACK.

train *v.* Multiple and continual climax with one woman during sexual intercourse. See PULL A TRAIN.

transvestite *n.* Male who obtains sexual gratification from dressing in female clothing.

trap *n.* (d) Hiding place for drugs. **a.k.a.** stash.

travel agent *n.* One who sells drugs. See PUSHER.

tread on me, don't See DON'T TREAD ON ME.

tree, out of one's See OUT OF ONE'S TREE.

trey *n.* (d) Three-dollar bag of heroin. See QUANTITIES OF DRUGS.

tric acid *n.* (d) High-quality LSD. See HALLUCINOGEN; LYSERGIC ACID DIETHYLAMIDE.

trick *v.* Participate in the sex act—eg. *I tricked with him.* See COPULATE. *n.* **1.** (pr) Man who pays for sexual relations with a prostitute. **a.k.a.** john. See FREAK TRICK. **2.** Female. See FEMALE.

trim *n.* (B) Sexual intercourse—eg. *Want some trim?* Originated in Harlem; almost obsolete. See COPULATION.

trip *v.* **1.** (d) Take a drug and get high. **a.k.a.** trip out

2. Think about; be mentally involved with; concentrate on—eg. *Was your mind tripping on her?* *n.* **1.** (d) Drug experience; activities done under the influence of a drug. **2.** Something out of the ordinary; an exciting or stimulating experience.

trip out *v.* **1.** (d) Get high on a drug. **a.k.a.** trip. **2.** Be out of touch with reality.

tripped out *adj.* Out of touch with reality.

tripper *n.* (d) One who takes drugs for the sole purpose of getting high.

tripping with death (d) Deliberately taking a drug or other substance that is very foreign to the body's chemical make-up and that one knows can result in death, eg., injecting pink lemonade (cleaning fluid) or inhaling ammonia mixed with Clorox.

trips *n.* (d) LSD. See HALLUCINOGEN; LYSERGIC ACID DIETHYLAMIDE.

trolley, conductor on the See CONDUCTOR ON THE TROLLEY.

trouble *n.* (h) A butch who is likely to cause trouble. See BUTCH.

truck driver *n.* (d) Amphetamine. See AMPHETAMINE.

T.S. Tough shit. Expression meaning too bad.

tuck and roll *v.* (d) Fold under instead of twist the paper ends of a marijuana cigarette. This is much more difficult than simply twisting the ends and is rarely done. **a.k.a.** New York tuck and roll. *n.* Style of car upholstery. *adj.* (d) Describes a marijuana cigarette whose ends have been folded under instead of twisted—eg. *These joints are tuck and roll.*

tuie (toó-e) *n.* (d) Tuinal; a barbiturate. Also spelled *tooie*. See BARBITURATE; TUINAL.

Tuinal *n.* (med) (amobarbital and secobarbital; Eli Lilly & Co) A barbiturate; combination of Amytal and Seconal that is a strong, long-acting hypnotic used to induce sleep. **a.k.a.** Christmas tree, double trouble, rainbow, red and blue, tooie, tootsie, tuie. See BARBITURATE.

tuna *n.* Female. See FEMALE.

tune in *v.* **1.** Focus on the action at hand. **2.** Become involved. See TUNE OUT.

tune out *v.* Ignore what is going on. See TUNE IN.

turkey *n.* **1.** Person unable to relate to people in a sociably acceptable manner. **2.** Non-narcotic powder sold as a narcotic. **a.k.a.** blank, dummy.

turkey, cold See COLD TURKEY.

turn a trick *v.* (pr) Perform sexual activities of any kind for profit. See TRICK.

turn off *v.* **1.** Be disinterested; be disgusted. **2.** Disgust (someone)—eg. *He turns me off.* **3.** Put someone out of a sexual mood. See TURN ON. **4.** Reject (someone).

turn on *v.* **1.** (d) Take drugs; get high, stoned. **2.** Introduce another to drugs. **a.k.a.** put on. **3.** Interest; attract (someone). **4.** Arouse sexual desire. See TURN OFF. **5.** (h) Become interested, get excited, and have sexual relations. **a.k.a.** turn over.

turn on to *v.* Begin to like; be interested in (things or people).

turn out *v.* **1.** Introduce someone to anything, eg., drugs. **2.** (pr) Get someone started in prostitution —eg. *Who turned you out?*

turn over *v.* (h) Become interested, get excited, and have sexual relations. **a.k.a.** turn on.

turnabout *n.* Change of one's mind or opinion—eg. *I did a real turnabout.* **a.k.a.** turnaround.

turnaround *n.* Change of one's mind or opinion—eg. *I did a real turnaround.* **a.k.a.** turnabout.

turned off *adj.* Disinterested; disgusted.

turned on *adj.* Under the influence of drugs. See LOADED.

turned on to *adj.* Interested.

turned out *adj.* **1.** Describes someone who has been introduced to anything, eg., drugs. **2.** (pr) Describes someone who has been started in prostitution.

turps *n.* (d) Elixir of terpin hydrate with cough syrup. Used to get high.

twat *n.* vagina. See VAGINA.

tweed *n.* (B) **1.** Clothes. **a.k.a.** vines. **2.** Well-dressed person.

twenty-five *n.* (d) LSD. Called twenty-five because that number is part of the full chemical name. **a.k.a.** 25. See HALLUCINOGEN; LYSERGIC ACID DIETHYLAMIDE.

T.W.H. Typically wavy hair.

twist *n.* (d) Marijuana cigarette. See MARIJUANA CIGARETTE.

twisted *adj.* **1.** (p) Received a jail sentence. See BUSTED BUT NOT TWISTED. **2.** (d) Under the influence of a drug. See LOADED.

u

U.M.A.S. United Mexican American Students.

Uncle Tom *n.* Black person who is passive, apologetic and subservient to whites. See TÍO TACO; TOM; UNCLE TOMMYHAWK.

Uncle Tommyhawk *n.* American Indian term for an Uncle Tom. See TÍO TACO; UNCLE TOM.

uncool *adj.* Unknowledgeable; not acting in a suave manner; not cool. See COOL.

uncut *adj.* (d) Pure form of a drug, not diluted. See CUT.

underground *adj.* Unsanctioned by prevailing social attitudes; anti-Establishment (see ESTABLISHMENT). For a long time the public was unaware of the subcultures of drug takers, hippies and sexual swingers (see SWINGER). Their existence was kept so quiet that they were called underground. They have influenced mainstream society a great deal; the growth of hair by hippies, beads by the mystic religious sects, clothes by homosexuals and hippies, advertising art by psychedelic art, and the moral code of today by all these groups, to mention only a few of the more obvious aspects. Examples of underground newspapers are the *Free Press* (Los Angeles) and *The Village Voice* (New York). Examples of underground movies are those of Andy Warhol. Many underground activities are now successful moneymaking ventures.

underground railway *n.* System that supplies food and lodging to runaway hippies.

unit *n.* An object. Usually refers to penis—eg. *She came in the door and grabbed my unit.* See PENIS.

up *n.* (d) Amphetamine. See AMPHETAMINE. *adj.* **1.** Happy; full of energy; full of life. **2.** (d) High on an amphetamine.

up front *adj.* Straightforward; open; truthful; honest; no false pretenses; "real people."

up tight *adj* **1.** In a state of extreme tension or great anxiety; worried; disturbed; upset. **a.k.a.** tight-assed. **2.** Inhibited—eg. *She is really up tight.* **a.k.a.** tight assed.

up your ass Expression meaning fuck you. See FUCK YOU.

upper *n.* (d) Amphetamine. See AMPHETAMINE.

uppie *n.* (d) Amphetamine. See AMPHETAMINE.

uppity *adj.* (B) Derogatory word usually used to describe a person who is obnoxious, stuck-up, bitchy or generally difficult to be with—eg. *You're really uppity today.* Women's Lib has a bumper sticker: "Uppity Women Unite."

V

vagina *n.* Female sex organ; canal leading from the vulva to the uterus. **a.k.a.** beaver, box, crack, cunt, hairburger, hairpie, nookie, pee hole, pussy, quim, slit, snapper, snatch, twat.

Valium *n.* (med) (diazepam; Roche Laboratories) Minor tranquilizer used in cases of anxiety and tension. Taken by dopers.

V.D. *n.* Venereal disease, eg., gonorrhea, syphilis.

vibe *v.* Send out vibrations (vibes)—eg. *He bad vibed me.* See VIBES.

vibes *n.* Vibrations feelings or thoughts that are transmitted non-verbally—eg. *I got good vibes from him.* See VIBE.

vibrations see VIBES.

vibrator *n.* Battery-operated vibrating device shaped similar to a penis. It can be inserted in the vagina to stimulate the inner area or can be used on the clitoris. It produces a very pleasurable orgasm. There are thinner, soft, plastic-coated vibrators for use in the anus. See DILDO.

vic *n.* Victim of a person who takes advantage of him and steals from him. See CON; CON GAME; HUSTLER.

vines *n.* Clothes. **a.k.a.** tweed.

vining *v.* Pertaining to the act of getting dressed. Comes from vines, which are clothes.

violate *v.* (p) Be returned to prison for a parole violation—eg. *I was violated.*

viper *n.* long-term marijuana user.

vitamin C *n.* (d) Vitamin-C tablet with a dot of LSD on it.

vodka acid *n.* (d) Mixture of vodka and LSD. Comes from acid, which means LSD.

vomit *v.* Regurgitate; throw up food the stomach rejects. **a.k.a.** dump, flash, heave, lose your cookies, ralph.

voyager *n.* (d) One who has taken LSD. Idea comes from trip, the LSD experience.

voyeur (voy-yər') *n.* One who obtains sexual gratification by viewing others engaged in any form of sexual activity; peeping Tom. *Voyeur* is French for "one who sees." **a.k.a.** picker.

W

wafer *n.* (d) Cookie that contains LSD.

wag out *v.* (d) Get high. See HIGH.

wail *v.* **1.** Do something well—eg. *He wails on that horn.* **2.** Have a good time—eg. *We were really wailing at the party.*

wake up *n.* (d) **1.** The first injection taken in the morning by an addict. **2.** Amphetamine. See AMPHETAMINE.

walk *v.* **1.** Leave; depart. **2.** Associate; get along with—eg. *He walks with many colors.* See LEAVE.

walk soft *v.* Be humble, not cocky; strong—eg. *I told him he was acting like an ass, and he walks a lot softer now.*

walking papers *n.* Release from any institution or contract.

wall, off the See OFF THE WALL.

wanna go out? (pr) Question used by prostitutes to ask a stranger if he wishes to engage in sexual relations (common in the eastern part of the U.S. and particularly New York).

want *n.* (p) Warrant for one's arrest.

washed up *adj.* (d) Withdrawn from drugs. See WITHDRAW.

wasp *n.* Stands for white Anglo-Saxon Protestant (the first letter of each word). Can be derogatory, meaning middle class, conservative, Republican, white American. See MISTER CHARLIE.

waste *v.* Hit very hard and hurt (someone).

wasted *adj.* **1.** (d) Totally or very much under the influence of a drug; extremely high. See LOADED. **2.** (d) Continuously on drugs. **3.** Drunk; high on alcohol. See LOADED. **4.** Emotionally or physically fatigued.

water pipe *n.* (d) Pipe for smoking marijuana, hashish or opium. Water filters the smoke; people often use wine instead of water. See HOOKAH.

watermelon head *n.* (B) Person who is from the country and not sophisticated in city ways. See COUNTRY.

way out *adj.* Beyond description. Can be both positive or negative—eg. *That chick is way out* (could mean great or awful). **a.k.a.** far out, freaky, kinky.

wedge *n.* (d) LSD. See HALLUCINOGEN; LYSERGIC ACID DIETHYLAMIDE.

weed head *n.* User of marijuana. See HEAD.

weed out *v.* (d) Smoke marijuana. Comes from weed, which is marijuana.

week-end habit *n.* (d) Small, irregular drug habit; person who uses drugs only on a week end.

weight *n.* (d) Measure or supply of drugs an addict needs in order to avoid withdrawal symptoms—eg. *I got my weight for the week*.

Wesson party *n.* Two or more people who get together to engage in sexual play and intercourse with their bodies covered with vegetable oil. This produces a unique sexual sensation. Comes from the brand name of the oil. **a.k.a.** Mazola party.

wham whams and zoo zoos *n.* (p) Penny candies that are purchased in prison canteens.

whang *n.* Penis. See PENIS.

whatever Expression meaning draw your own conclusions; passive response to avoid making statements or decisions; expression used frequently by passive people. **a.k.a.** I don't know.

what's been going down Expression meaning occurrences, happenings, events—eg. *can't take what's been going down*.

what's happening? 1 Form of salutation meaning what's going on? or how are you? **2.** (d) Drug users' way of identifying themselves as such to any strangers suspected of being users.

wheels *n.* **1.** Car. See CAR. **2.** Any form of transportation.

where is it with you? Question usually asked to determine a person's emotional state.

where it's at The locus or center of a situation—eg. *This is where it's at.* **a.k.a.** nitty gritty.

whip it to me! expression used (1) to ask for or have sexual intercourse or (2) to say that someone is really performing well sexually. **a.k.a.** sock it to me!

whipped *adj.* Very tired; exhausted. **a.k.a.** wiped out.

whipped cream *n.* **1.** (d) The gas used in whipped-cream cans is sniffed to get high. The cream is left to settle, then the lever is depressed just enough to allow only the gas to escape into the mouth. This practice can easily and quickly cause death. **2.** Whipped cream may be used in sexual activity for variety—put on another's body and licked off, as illustrated on the album cover of the Tijuana Brass's recording called "Whipped Cream and Other Delights."

whipping, I'm See I'M WHIPPING.

whippo *n., adj.* Word that can be or describe anything. It derives its meaning from the context of the sentence, voice inflection or facial expression. The word was originated by California disc jockey Dick Whittington—eg. *Whittington is whippo!*

white *n.* (d) **1.** Heroin. Comes from the color of the drug. See HEROIN. **2.** Amphetamine See AMPHETAMINE. **3.** Benzedrine. See BENZEDRINE.

white drugs *n.* Cocaine. Term not used by addicts. See COCAINE.

white lady, the *n.* (d) Heroin. See HEROIN.

white lightning *n.* (d) LSD with a lot of Methedrine.

white paddy *n.* Derogatory term for a white person. See PADDY.

white spot *n.* (B) White person who associates only with Black people.

white stuff *n.* (d) **1.** Heroin. See HEROIN. **2.** Morphine. See MORPHINE. **3.** Cocaine. See COCAINE.

whitey *n.* (B) **1.** White person. See GRINGO. **2.** The Es-

tablishment. See ESTABLISHMENT; MISTER CHARLIE.
whitie *n.* (d) Amphetamine. See AMPHETAMINE.
whore *n.* Prostitute. See PROSTITUTE.
wicked *adj.* Out of the ordinary; very pleasing; groovy. See GROOVY.
wife *n.* Female spouse. **a.k.a.** better half, hope to die, main squeeze, old lady, piece, woman.
wig *v.* Get upset or excited. Comes from head or hair, which can then mean the mind. See LOSE ONE'S WIG.
wig out *v.* **1.** Lose control of one's senses. **2.** Have an emotional experience, not necessarily associated with drugs. **3.** Suddenly surprise another. **4.** Get very excited about someone or something. **a.k.a.** flip, flip out.
wigged out *adj.* **1.** No longer in control of one's senses. **2.** Very excited about someone or something. **a.k.a.** flipped out.
wiggy *adj.* Wild; cool; fantastic; fun; groovy. See GROOVY.
wind, get in the See GET IN THE WIND.
wind (it) out *v.* Take off very fast in a car.
winder *n.* One who voluntarily enters a hospital to take a cure to stop using drugs. See CURE, THE; LEXINGTON.
wipe out *v.* **1.** Win over or beat someone. **2.** End; stop; close.
wiped *adj.* Killed. **a.k.a.** wiped out.
wiped out *adj.* **1.** Tired; exhausted. **a.k.a.** whipped. **2.** Destroyed; wrecked; hurt. **3.** Killed. **a.k.a.** wiped. **4.** State of having lost all one's money and/or possessions. **5.** Totally under the influence of a drug. See LOADED.
wired *adj.* **1.** (d) High on a drug. See LOADED. **2.** (d) The feeling of never being able to sleep again; very on edge; very awake; usually happens while taking uppers. **3.** Up; high (not on a drug); excited; happy. **a.k.a.** jacked up. **4.** Very nervous. **a.k.a.** jacked up.

wise up *v.* Become aware; know what's happening; find out about.

wisher *n.* (d) Federal narcotics agent **a.k.a.** fuzz, narc, narco, sam. See FED.

withdraw *v.* (d) Stop using a physically addictive drug. **a.k.a.** clear up, take a cure.

withdrawal *n.* (d) Physical reactions that occur when a person addicted to a drug stops using that drug. The symptoms are stomach contractions and pains, tearing of the eyes, runny nose, vomiting, muscle contractions and aching in general. Symptoms are most common in withdrawal from opiates—eg. heroin, morphine—but also occur in withdrawal from alcohol and barbiturates. Sometimes people try to control these symptoms by giving increasingly smaller doses of the drug, weaning the person. See CURE, THE; LEXINGTON.

wolf *v.* Criticize; chop down. *n.* Man who is overly forward and pressing with his flirtation.

Women's Lib Women's Liberation.

won't quit Expression meaning to continue; fail to stop—eg. *That drug won't quit.*

work *v.* (pr) Solicit or have intercourse—eg. *Were you working today?* See COPULATE.

work out! Expression meaning (1) to manifestly express oneself to the fullest extent of one's abilities or (2) to really be involved in an action and feel it to the fullest.

work over *v.* **1.** Beat up physically **2.** Harass mentally.

work (someone) *v.* Manipulate; take advantage of—eg. *She worked me for the use of my car.* See CON.

working for me Expression describing something beneficial, useful to one.

working girl *n.* (pr) Prostitute. See PROSTITUTE.

works *n.* (d) Equipment used for preparing and injecting drugs. See FIT.

wow Exclamation of bewilderment or excitement—eg. *Wow!!! Are you serious?*

Wrinkle-room *n.* (h) Homosexual bar (gay bar) frequented by aging homosexuals.

wrongheadedness *n.* Stupidity.

Wyamine (wī'-ə-min) *n.* (med) (mephentermine; Wyeth Laboratories) An amphetamine; upper. Wyamine can be purchased in any drugstore over the counter with no prescription necessary. It comes in an inhaler. Drug users unscrew the bottom of the inhaler, take out the cotton and either draw the solution into a syringe and inject it or take it orally. The effects are similar to those of LSD but without the hallucinations. See AMPHETAMINE.

X

X Sign painted on walls by gangs. It means that this is gang territory. The X is often accompanied by names or initials of gangs and gang members. The sign can also mean the place where one gang meets or where two gangs will meet and fight. (See RUMBLE). This sign is used by people of junior and senior high school age.

y

yancy *adj.* Nervous; restless. **a.k.a.** antsy.

yedo (*Spanish* ye-do') *n.* Marijuana. See MARIJUANA.

yellow *n.* (d) **1.** Nembutal; a downer, or barbiturate. Comes from its color. See BARBITURATE; NEMBUTAL. **2.** LSD. **a.k.a.** orange, sunshine. See LSD.

yellow football *n.* (d) Type of very strong synthetic mescaline. **a.k.a.** pumpkin seed. See MESCALINE.

yellow jacket *n.* (d) Nembutal; a downer, or barbiturate. Comes from its color. See BARBITURATE; NEMBUTAL.

yen *n.* **1.** (d) Desire for drugs. **2.** Desire for sexual intercourse.

yen hook *n.* Instrument (pipe) used in opium smoking.

yen shee *n.* Opium ash.

yen shee suey *n.* Opium wine.

yen sleep *n.* Drowsy, restless state during the period of withdrawal from drugs. See WITHDRAWAL.

yesca (*Spanish* yes'-kah) *n.* Marijuana. See MARIJUANA.

yippie *n.* Person associated with the Youth International Party; a hippy idea of activities. The yippies gained publicity from their activities at the Democratic Convention in Chicago in 1968. Their symbol is Y, which is written on walls.

yippy See YIPPIE.

you know (ya' know) Expression commonly used in conversation, intermittent with what one is say ing. Used frequently by drug addicts.

youngblood *n.* (d) A young person starting out on marijuana.

Y.S.A. *n.* Young Socialist Alliance. Marxist-Leninist youth group; Trotskyite. Its members are in favor of the overthrow of the capitalist system, wanting to replace it with a Marxist-Leninist-Trotskyite socialist system.

Z

zap Exclamation used to indicate movement, action, change of scene. Usually said three times. *v.* **1.** Present something in an indelibly memorable way so as to produce a change—eg. *Zap the world with love.* **2.** Kill someone. **a.k.a.** rip off, snuff, take off, zonk.

zebra *adj.* Racially mixed (Black and white) couple or group.

Zen *n.* **1.** (d) LSD. It is called Zen because it is alleged to give the same type of insights and revelations that are associated with Zen. See HALLUCINOGEN; LYSERGIC ACID DIETHYLAMIDE. **2.** Zen Buddhism is an Eastern religion currently popular in the West. It leads to a state of consciousness that is associated with attaining self-awareness, enlightenment and insight.

Zig Zag *n.* (d) Brand name for cigarette papers used in rolling one's own cigarettes with marijuana or tobacco.

Zig Zag man *n.* (d) Symbol that is on the cover of the Zig Zag cigarette papers' package. It is a man smoking a cigarette.

zit *n.* Pimple.

ZNA *n.* (d) Dill weed smoked to obtain a high.

zonk *v.* Kill someone. **a.k.a.** rip off, snuff, take off, zap.

zonked *adj.* (d) So completely high on a drug that the individual is non-functional. **a.k.a.** zonked out.

zonked out *adj.* (d) So completely high on a drug that the individual is non-functional. **a.k.a.** zonked.

zoom *n.* (d) Amphetamine; an upper. Usually refers to Methedrine. See AMPHETAMINE; METHEDRINE.

numbers

½ can *n.* Amount of narcotics equal to half a Prince Albert tobacco can. **a.k.a.** half can, matchbox. See QUANTITIES OF DRUGS.

2-13 *n.* Drug addict.

4-F Meaning find them, feel them, fuck them and forget them. Used to describe certain type of man who is only interested in a very casual relationship with little or no involvement—eg. *He's a 4-F-er.*

8 *n.* (d) Heroin. Comes from H, which is the eighth letter of the alphabet. See HEROIN.

8 to 5 *n.* A mundane, everyday job.

10¢ bag *n.* (d) Ten-dollar quantity of a drug. **a.k.a** dime bag, ten-cent bag. See QUANTITIES OF DRUGS.

13 *n.* (d) Marijuana. M is the 13th letter of the alphabet. See MARIJUANA.

14 *n.* (d) Narcotics. N is the 14th letter of the alphabet.

25 *n.* (d) LSD. Comes from d-lysergic acid diethylamide tartrate 25, the chemical name. See HALLUCINOGEN; LYSERGIC ACID DIETHYLAMIDE.

69 *v.* Oral-genital copulation between two partners, both orally caressing each other simultaneously. Comes from the similarity of the position to the number 69. **a.k.a.** flip flop. See LOOP-DE-LOOP; ORAL COPULATION.

symbols

Female.

Male.

Ankh (ahnk) Egyptian symbol of fertility.

Peace symbol. It originated in England with the nuclear disarmament organization that sponsored the Aldermasten peace marches at Easter.

A button with a capital S on it stands for socialism. The wearer is in favor of a movement toward socialism.

Holding first and middle fingers in shape of a V with the nails toward yourself means peace.

Holding first and middle fingers in shape of a V with the nails toward the other person means fuck you. See FUCK YOU.

symbols 206

Holding middle finger up while bending others means fuck you. See FUCK YOU.

Symbol of Ecology Action, a political organization that educates and lobbies to save the environment.

The flag of ecology bears the Greek letter theta (which is traditionally a warning of death) and is the banner symbolizing the threatened environment. Its stripes, thirteen in number, are green for unspoiled land and white for clean air.

The theta symbol alone also represents the ecology commitment to restore the earth waters and atmosphere to a non-pol luted state.